WRITE
Is a
VERB

WRITE
Is a
VERB

Sit Down.
Start Writing.
No Excuses.

Bill O'Hanlon

WRITER'S DIGEST BOOKS
Cincinnati, Ohio
www.writersdigest.com

To receive a free weekly e-mail newsletter delivering tips and updates about writing and about Writer's Digest products, register directly at our Web site at http://newsletters.fwpublications.com.

11 10 09 08 07   5 4 3 2 1

Distributed in Canada by Fraser Direct, 100 Armstrong Avenue, Georgetown, Ontario, Canada L7G 5S4, Tel: (905) 877-4411; Distributed in the U.K. and Europe by David & Charles, Brunel House, Newton Abbot, Devon, TQ12 4PU, England, Tel: (+44) 1626 323200, Fax: (+44) 1626 323319, E-mail: postmaster@davidandcharles.co.uk; Distributed in Australia by Capricorn Link, P.O. Box 704, Windsor, NSW 2756 Australia, Tel: (02) 4577-3555

Library of Congress Cataloging-in-Publication Data

O'Hanlon, William Hudson.
   Write is a verb : Sit down. Start writing. No excuses / By Bill O'Hanlon.
        p. cm.
   Includes index.
   ISBN-13: 978-1-58297-459-0 (hardcover : alk. paper)
   ISBN-10: 1-58297-459-4 (hardcover : alk. paper)
   1. Authorship. I. Title.
   PN147O33 2007
   808.02--dc22   2007015564

Edited by Jane Friedman
Designed by Eric West and Grace Ring
Cover designed by Eric West
DVD video by CineVision Productions & Media
DVD menus by Jen Rizzo
DVD music by Flying Hands Music
Production coordinated by Mark Griffin

F+W PUBLICATIONS, INC.

Dedication

To Steffanie and The Biscuit,
who are my verbs, my nouns,
and my plus perfects. To my
son, Patrick, who has taught
me a lot about persistence and
hanging in there.

Acknowledgments

Thanks go to: Faith Hamlin, agent extraordinaire and kind soul, for helping to bring this project to print; Jane Friedman for suggesting the project and shepherding it along to completion (and for letting me sit in on the title meeting—I enjoyed it; great staff); all my writing students and clients, who taught me a lot about what works and what doesn't and how people write and get motivated in such diverse ways; all my editors through the years, notably Susan Munro, formerly of W.W. Norton, who taught me so much about writing with her gentle and effective editing with my first twelve books; and my wife Steffanie, who helped me curb my ADHD tendencies and aim for something better than "good enough."

About the Author

Bill O'Hanlon, M.S., LMFT, has authored or coauthored twenty-eight books, including *Change 101* (W.W. Norton, 2006), *Pathways to Spirituality* (W.W. Norton, 2006), and *Thriving Through Crisis* (Penguin/Perigee, 2005; winner of a Books for a Better Life Award, 2005).

He has published fifty-four articles or book chapters. His books have been translated into sixteen languages: French, Spanish, Portuguese, Swedish, Finnish, German, Chinese, Bulgarian, Turkish, Korean, Indonesian, Italian, Croatian, Arabic, Polish, and Japanese. He has appeared on *Oprah* (with his book *Do One Thing Different*), *The Today Show*, and a variety of other TV and radio programs.

Since 1977, Bill has given over two thousand talks around the world. He has been a top-rated speaker at many international conferences and was awarded the Outstanding Mental Health Educator of the Year award in 2001 by the New England Educational Institute.

Bill is a Licensed Mental Health Professional, Certified Professional Counselor, and a Licensed Marriage and Family Therapist. He regularly speaks about writing and offers intensive seminars for people who want to write books and get them published.

Visit Bill online at www.billohanlon.com or (for more on his writing coaching and instruction) www.getyourbook written.com.

CONTENTS

CHAPTER 3

Do One Thing Different   52

Changing one small thing to get your writing done.

CHAPTER 4

Baby Steps, Baby Steps   74

The small-steps method for getting your writing done.

CHAPTER 5

The Promise Method   89

Using commitments to get your writing done.

CHAPTER 6

The Solution-Oriented Method   103

Revisiting what has worked to get your writing done.

CHAPTER 7

Anything Worth Doing
Is Worth Doing Poorly   123

Embracing mistakes, failure, and
imperfection to get your writing done.

CHAPTER 8

It's Not About You, It's All About You 132

Taking the focus off yourself to overcome writer's block and other barriers to writing.

CHAPTER 9

Clueless in Publishing Land 138

Three crucial tips for getting published.

CHAPTER 10

Common Writing Poisons and Their Antidotes 184

How to challenge unhelpful ideas or attitudes that will kill your writing dreams and ambitions.

Index   201

About the DVD   212

INTRO

I always wanted to be an author and be published. I figured the way to do that was to write a book.

—STEVE MARTIN

I have written more than twenty books and fifty-four book chapters or articles. People often ask me how I write so much. I actually consider myself a bit of a slacker—rather lazy and undisciplined. Isaac Asimov wrote more than five hundred books before his death in 1992. English novelist John Creasey wrote 562 books over his forty-year career. Dame Barbara Cartland wrote more than seven hundred romance novels. Compared to these folks, I *am* a slacker. I have many more ideas for books yet to write, and if I had known some of the material in this book earlier in my writing career, I would now have many more books completed and published.

When I began writing, I was more of a thinker than a doer. I believe I'm the right person to write this book because I'm not a "natural" writer and writing certainly didn't come easy for me. It was like blood on the keyboard with my early books—struggling to get myself to write and to keep writing. The writing, when it finally appeared on the page, was unsatisfying—stilted and flat. I love good writing, and I wasn't even coming close. But I soldiered on, and through the years writing has become less torturous and, finally, actually enjoyable at times. The thing that carried me through the early years was a burning passion to express myself in print and to help others.

I was trained as a psychotherapist (with the emphasis on the *psycho*, I often say). I helped people make changes in difficult circumstances for more than thirty years before I began full-time writing and speaking, so I have learned something about how to motivate people to take action and change until the desired result appears.

For the past few years I have led book writing and publishing boot camps in Santa Fe, where I live. These intense seminars are designed to help people write the book, or books, they want to write and get them published.

It's been an interesting experience to observe the people who have attended these seminars, both those who have followed through and gotten their books written and published, and those who haven't. I began to notice patterns of what works to get book projects written and what doesn't,

2

and which people published their projects and which didn't (or haven't yet—some are still in process). Some people are amazingly fast and committed once they get some coaching, encouragement, and information. Others are slow and steady and get it done eventually. Still others are a study in how *not* to write a book.

I have read a lot of books with advice from writers about the best way to write or get oneself to write. They often provide rules. Write on a schedule; write in a special place, undisturbed by ringing telephones or people; write a certain number of words or pages each day; write standing up; write in a café surrounded by people; don't show your writing to anyone; show your writing to a trusted friend; don't talk about your writing as it will rob the energy from it; write every day; write with a special pen in a special notebook; outline before you write; and so on. These rules are based on things that have worked for those writers.

I have never followed any of these rules and here I am on my twenty-somethingth book. In the end, you have to find what works for you, not what works for someone else. Having said that, there are some general principles that can make you more likely to get your stuff written and completed, and that's what I'll offer in this book. No rules: There are guidelines and hints, ideas, and methods that you can personalize to your style and preferences—but you won't find *rules*.

As I said, I have read a lot of books about writing— and I have never found the help I have put in this book.

I have combined my experience as a therapist and with helping people make difficult changes in their lives, then added what I have learned from my own writing career and from the people I have taught and coached, and put it all into this book you're holding. I have tried to make it practical, fun, and motivational. My purpose is to get you moving, get you writing, and impel you to get your writing projects completed and published. I will use the literary equivalents of Prozac, cattle prods, M&Ms, and whatever else I need to get you off the dime and help you get your book written.

If you read this book and merely come away having enjoyed the read, I will consider it a failure. I expect to receive many signed copies of books in the coming years from all of you who have finally gotten off the dime and written your books.

One more quotation (source unknown) to give you a kick in the pants: "The trouble with doing nothing is you never know when you're finished."

Okay, enough hooptedoodle and introduction. Let's get cracking.

Key Points

- You don't have to be a natural writer or a good writer to write; you just have to write.

- It's important to find your own style and motivation—everyone is different.

- This book will give you guidelines, encouragement, and strategies to get yourself to write and to sustain the writing to complete projects.

The Juice

Finding the energy to write.

Everyone should carefully observe which way his heart draws him, and then choose that way with all his strength.

—HASIDIC SAYING

The process of writing a book usually takes a lot of energy. You have to sustain your enthusiasm through the various processes of writing and editing, as well as the selling and marketing that follows publication.

In the movie *Jerry Maguire*, the sports star (played by Cuba Gooding, Jr.) tells agent Jerry (played by Tom Cruise), "Show me the money." But he didn't just say it; he repeated it, shouted it, got his family to say it, danced to it, and made Jerry scream it at the top of his lungs until he (Gooding, Jr.) felt the point had gotten across—it was that important.

I will say something similar in regard to writing: *Show me the energy*. In this chapter I'll give you a clear set of guidelines for discovering and tapping into the energy that can sustain you through the writing and publishing process.

Show Me the Energy

Lee Boudreaux, once a senior editor at Random House, spoke of the need for energy in the writing and publishing process, in *The Making of a Bestseller*:

> Passion for a book is like an electrical impulse traveling down a wire, and that electrical impulse has to be strong enough to affect a lot of people, from the writer to the agent to the editor. Then from the editor to the publicist who needs to get the book reviewed, the art director who is responsible for coming up with the right cover, the sales reps who sell the book to the store buyers. Then from the store's main buyer to the individual booksellers and, eventually, to the customer.

Jane Smiley, in a 2006 interview with *Writer's Digest* magazine, also emphasized the need for energy in writing a book:

> You have to have a lot of energy and conviction to propel yourself through the writing of a novel, because it often takes a year, two years, or more. So the interest has to be a compelling one. And lots of times the reason the subject is compelling is because you have passionate convictions about it. Most prolific writers are, by nature, people of

passionate ideas, but the particular ideas that make them passionate tend to come and go over the years. They keep going by taking up new ideas with the same passion.

Dennis Palumbo was a successful TV and motion picture writer (he wrote, among other things, the movie *My Favorite Year*, the first episode of *The Love Boat*, and some episodes of *Welcome Back, Kotter*). He was also in therapy. Palumbo enjoyed the therapy process a great deal and, finding himself increasingly interested in therapy, volunteered to co-facilitate a group for seriously mentally ill patients. One day during a script meeting, he caught himself glancing impatiently at his watch, wondering when the meeting would be over and whether he could make it across town to his therapy group on time. At that moment, he realized he would rather be a therapist. (I know, I know; many people would kill to be in his shoes, at a TV script meeting in Hollywood.) The point is: He followed his energy and became a therapist. The same goes for writing. Follow your energy.

It's a bad idea to write a book just to write it (and if you are writing a book to get rich and famous, you may need some antipsychotic drugs, as few writers actually make a full-time living at their writing; still fewer become rich and famous). I read once of a would-be writer who asked Henry Miller (author of *Tropic of Cancer*) how he should go about deciding whether to be a writer. Miller replied, "If you can't *not* be a writer, then be a writer."

I feel the same way about writing books. If you decide you could skip writing it, don't bother. The book should be compelling enough for you that it *has* to be written. That requires energy.

My journey through the world of writing and publishing illustrates very well this element of writing. There is no way I would have written my books without a deep and abiding passion.

My Story

I was depressed when I was a young adult and came close to committing suicide. A friend talked me out of it, but realized I had to do something about how depressed and unhappy I had become. I became obsessed with discovering how to become less miserable, and in the process, stumbled on the field of psychotherapy. Initially studying it just for myself, I discovered many useful tools that helped me feel better and improved my relationships with others. After a time, I decided to make the field of psychotherapy my career and earned a graduate degree. I loved the field of therapy—honorable work helping relieve people from their suffering, sometimes literally saving lives. I practiced as a therapist from 1974 to 2004.

Then I came across some of my colleagues who didn't share my enthusiasm or optimism about the possibilities for change in people. I heard them say things that seemed blasphemy to me: *None of my patients really want to change. They love being miserable. They are just playing a game with me. The only person who likes change is a wet baby.*

Particularly galling was the fact that most of these discouraged and discouraging therapists hadn't bothered to keep up on the latest developments in the field. They had some outdated ideas and methods, and when their clients didn't respond to these ineffective approaches, they would decide the person was "resistant" or unable to change. I constantly read the latest books and attended training courses and was excited to find something that might help my clients more quickly and effectively. When I tried to encourage these therapists to read more or attend training courses, they dismissed me as a novice who didn't know what he was talking about.

Therapists, like practitioners in most fields, listen to experts. I realized that, if I were going to influence them, I would have to become an expert myself to gain credibility. I began to teach seminars, which led to requests for my teachings in book form.

A book? I didn't have time to write. I was busy earning a living and raising a family. I wasn't very good at writing and found the process torturous. I would have some ideas when I sat down to write, and they would come out onto the page only with great difficulty, and even then the words would be flat and lifeless. I loved good writing, and I could see that mine sucked. But I persisted because I was so angry about what was happening in my field. I wanted everyone to know there was a better way to approach change.

It turned out there was a receptive and eager audience and my books began to sell. I wrote more. It still wasn't easy, but I gained confidence and that helped. I spent most of my writing time rewriting (I rewrote my first book thirty-five times!) because I found that rewriting made the writing, if not good, at least clear. Finally, after a number of books, I began to enjoy the writing process, and it came more easily. I found my voice. I discovered what worked for me in my writing process.

The point? I wouldn't have ever written a book without a passion for my subject. I loved psychotherapy. I thought it was an important and sacred field. Then I got angry about the cavalier and discouraging attitude some of my colleagues had regarding the possibilities and likelihood of change. That righteous anger fueled my writing.

Science fiction author Ray Bradbury wrote, in *Zen in the Art of Writing*, "... [if I were] asked to name the most important items in a writer's make-up, the things that shape his material and rush him along the road to where he wants to go, I could only warn him to look to his zest, to see his gusto."

How do you find or connect with the gusto and zest—also known as the juice—that will fuel your writing through the book creation and publishing process? By identifying and connecting with one or more of the four writing energies.

The Four Writing Energies

I believe there are four energies that drive the writing process: blissed, blessed, dissed, and pissed (two are "positive" and two "negative"—guess which are which!).

POSITIVE ENERGIES

Writers can be blissed (excited or passionate about their subjects or the writing process itself) or blessed (encouraged by someone who believes in them or their writing abilities, or just in the right place at the right time). When these positive energies are released, they can fuel a book or a lifetime of writing.

Blissed is the excited, passionate love or fascination for some activity or subject. Some writers just love to write. Others are fascinated with the subject of their writing. Some are obsessed with or taken over by characters or the research they do for the book.

Jane Smiley again, from her book *Thirteen Ways of Looking at the Novel*:

> The desire to write a novel is the single required prerequisite for writing a novel. It is the only thing that overcomes all the handicaps—perfectionism, low self-esteem, depression, alcoholism, diseases of all kinds, immense riches, economic hardship, deadly enemies, the resistance of relatives and friends, laziness, retarded professional development, the regular responsibilities of adulthood, even imprisonment (Sir Thomas Malory, for example, wrote the romance/protonovel *Le Morte D'Arthur* while imprisoned during the War of the Roses). While the desire to write a novel does not guarantee that the resulting novel will be a good one, or, if it is, that the author will produce a string of good ones, it is the only way to begin.

And from writer Annie Dillard, in her essay "Fashioning a Text":

Writing a book is like rearing children—willpower has very little to do with it. If you have a little baby crying in the middle of the night, and if you depend only on willpower to get you out of bed to feed the baby, that baby will starve. You do it out of love. Willpower is a weak idea; love is strong. You don't have to scourge yourself with a cat-o'-nine-tails to go to the baby. You go to the baby out of love for that particular baby. That's the same way you go to your desk. There's nothing freakish about it. Caring passionately about something isn't against nature, and it isn't against human nature. It's what we're here to do.

Filmmaker George Lucas refers to this bliss energy when he said: "You have to find something that you love enough to be able to take risks, jump over the hurdles, and break through the brick walls that are always going to be placed in front of you. If you don't have that kind of feeling for what it is you're doing, you'll stop at the first giant hurdle."

Blessed is the energy released when someone encourages you in your writing life or believes in your promise as a writer. It might be a high school English teacher, or a mentor in the form of another writer.

I was blessed by a colleague of mine early in my career. When he asked what I was up to, I excitedly related my plans about challenging the therapy world and the books I was writing. He listened silently and then uttered seven words so affirming they gave me confidence and energy for years when I thought back to them: "Bill," he said, "I think you're up to something big." When my energy would flag or people would criticize my writing, I would remember his faith and belief in me and get right back on the horse.

Paranormal mystery writer Charlaine Harris was blessed by her second husband when he gave her an electric typewriter on their wedding day and said, "I know you've always wanted to write. Try staying home and writing the book you've always wanted to write." She avoided writing for a few months and he gently prodded her to get to it. She began and has turned out many successful novels. Not all writers are blessed with such encouraging partners.

Another way to be blessed is to be in the right place at the right time. One of my inspirations in the therapy field was an eccentric and gifted psychiatrist named Milton Erickson. I just happened to be working at an art gallery at my university when he arrived to buy something. After he left, a fellow student showed me an article about him, which just happened to have been on the desk in the gallery. I read the article and was fascinated.

I ended up being a student of Erickson's in the years before his death in 1980 and later wrote several books about his work. He blessed me by providing me with encouragement and confidence, as well as an exciting and fulfilling topic on which to write and speak. I couldn't stop telling Erickson stories to everyone I knew. Erickson was deliberately confusing in how he taught and wrote, and rarely explained how he did therapy, so it fell to me and his other students to write and teach about his work when interest in his ideas grew after his death. This led to my first published book, called *Taproots*, which attempted to explain and make clear what Erickson did.

Blessed is meeting an editor or an agent unexpectedly. You might see something, read something, or hear something that gives you inspiration for a book project. My first book contract came about as a result of a colleague having told a book publisher that I was an expert on a certain area of psychotherapy and that I knew the up-and-coming writers in that area. In the course of our brief meeting over drinks, after I told the publisher who was "hot" in the area, I casually mentioned that I was planning to write some books as well. He asked what they were about and one of them caught his interest. He suggested I write him a proposal and, within weeks, I had a book contract.

Of course, you can do some things to make your own luck (as the saying goes, "I'm a great believer in luck. I find that the harder I work, the luckier I get"). Going to the Iowa Writers' Workshop is no guarantee of success for a writer, but it does seem to increase the odds. Going to writers conferences, as long as you don't use it as a substitute for writing or get discouraged in the process, puts you in the way of several circumstances that might lead to blessings in your writing life. Call it serendipity or being blessed or working hard to get luckier. When it happens, it can sometimes release the writer in you.

So writers can be blissed or blessed ... but positive energy is only half the energy story.

NEGATIVE ENERGIES

Writing can be like photography: You can use the negative to develop. For many writers, the energies that drive their work come from a negative motivation—they are so upset, angry, or unhappy that they feel compelled to express those emotions through writing. Or they want to prove someone wrong, or right some injustice in the world through their writing.

Dissed is the category of negative energies that includes the experiences of being wounded emotionally, cursed or put down by others, or disrespected or rejected.

Take the story of writer Dominick Dunne. He was a Hollywood producer, doing relatively all right. But after some years at it, he realized even though he had minor fame and success, he didn't really *like* the life he thought he would love. He began to drink to excess and use drugs, and got fired. "Thank God I hit bottom," he said, "Hitting bottom is a wonderful thing. ... If you can get back up."

Then a scandal erupted in Hollywood. A producer, David Begelman, was found to have forged a ten-thousand-dollar check in the name of actor Cliff Robertson (it was later discovered that Begelman had forged forty thousand dollars in checks to cover gambling debts). Dunne followed the story in the papers and, having time on his hands, became obsessed with it. But the local papers soon swept it under the rug. Hollywood closed ranks and protected one of its own. *The Washington Post* got wind of the cover-up and sent two investigative reporters to Hollywood, but they couldn't get the close-knit Hollywood community to open up about the story.

When one of them spotted Dunne in a restaurant (the reporter had gone to school with Dunne's brother, writer John Gregory Dunne), Dunne—unemployed, with time on his hands, interested in the story, and knowing all the players in Hollywood—agreed to get the reporters entree into the Hollywood community. For two weeks, he accompanied them on their investigation. As he saw what investigative reporters did, he thought to himself, "I can do this." He'd always had the idea in the back of his mind that he would like to write, and here was a direction.

Two other things made the direction much more clear. One was that Begelman essentially got away with few consequences from his misdeed (he was fired as head of one big studio but soon hired as head of another), while Robertson, the victim, never had a major role in Hollywood after that. This mystified and upset Dunne.

The other clarifying moment was the brutal murder of Dunne's daughter. Dunne attended the trial and was appalled to see that the murderer seemed to have been coached on what to wear and how to act (he carried a Bible and read it constantly during the trial). Dunne, from his time in the movies, could recognize acting and props when he saw them. His outrage grew as the trial proceeded and it became clear to him that not everyone suffers the same legal consequences for bad deeds as the rest of us.

Then a light came on. He realized he could spend the rest of his life angry and embittered—or he could become an investigative reporter, specializing in writing about the rich and powerful in legal settings. (Dunne combined his outrage at miscarriages of justice with his fascination with the rich and famous.) "I had never had an interest in justice," he declared. "I was the guy who would rather be at the party." But now he was obsessed with justice. He left Hollywood and moved to a one-room cabin in Oregon to write. He's made a good living at it ever since and has illuminated the injustice that occurs when the rich and powerful are able to get away with murder because of their fame, wealth, and connections. He certainly was blissed about writing, but the initial energy came from being upset and wounded.

Best-selling writer Anne Rice lost her five-year-old daughter to leukemia. She completed the first book in her series of vampire novels the year after her daughter's death and made one of the main vampire characters a very young girl—a five-year-old who could never die. She could have taken to her bed and given up on life, but she transformed the energy and pain of grief into writing.

Author Andrew Solomon, who has written one of the best-selling books on depression, *The Noonday Demon*, explained his motivation this way, in an article from *Book* magazine in July/August 2002: "I had a breakdown. And then, having had one, I looked around and tried to find a book that I felt would be really helpful to me. I had a sense of what would be most helpful, and I felt it wasn't there. So, as I recovered from my depression, I felt more and more that there was a need for such a book and that I knew how to write one." His wound—being profoundly depressed—led to his writing life.

In order to have your wound or someone's curse fuel your writing process, the hurt or negative energy needs to be turned into creative energy, informing or driving your writing. It's not enough to be wounded; you must find a way to turn that wound into energy for your writing. Otherwise, you would just withdraw from life or risk, as many of my psychotherapy clients had done when they sought my help.

Somehow writers, even if they are not all mentally or emotionally healthy, have found a way to transmute their hurts into productive writing. Sometimes this writing helps to heal the hurts; other times the hurt never heals but continues to fuel the writer's creative life, thus resulting in some meaning being derived from the pain. This meaning itself can be healing, even if the original pain remains.

Make no mistake. I have seen screeds full of anger, self-pity, or hate that I think will never (and should never) be published. They are simply expressions of the author's pain, more like a journal entry than a book. They are self-indulgent and should be kept private because they have no public utility. In order to turn that pain and anger into a book, the writing needs to somehow turn the personal into the universal. It needs to be written well and transmuted into something that contributes and speaks to others.

Pissed is similar to dissed in that it often arises from disrespect or upset, but it manifests more as anger and righteous indignation than hurt. I have found that pissed usually arises from being upset about some social injustice or incompetence, rather than personal injury.

EXERCISE 1: FIND THE JUICE

- What are you passionate about?

- What do you care about so deeply or get so excited about that you talk about it to anyone who will listen?

- Do you love the process of writing itself?

- Who has encouraged your writing?

- Who would be proved wrong if you wrote and succeeded with your writing?

- Who has criticized, cursed, or discouraged you to the extent that it makes you want to prove them wrong?

- What upsets you so much that you are compelled to write about it or include the theme in your book?

- When have you (or someone you cared about) been disrespected in a way that makes you want to write?

- Where have you been lucky enough to be in the right place at the right time in regard to your writing?

- What could you do to increase the odds of being lucky in respect to finding inspiration?

- What are you afraid to write but know is a deep truth?

- Who are you afraid will disapprove of your writing or be upset by it?

- What are you afraid will happen if you write?

- What fears could you write and perhaps work through by writing?

I was first inspired to begin my public speaking career, even though I was shy, after attending and paying for a workshop with a speaker who didn't know his subject and wasn't prepared. I didn't have much money at the time and was annoyed. I wasn't really hurt or wounded, but I was *pissed*. I ranted all the way home to one of my colleagues and then, after arriving home, to my roommate. My roommate turned to me and said, "Well, if you think *you* could do a better job, why don't you present workshops?" It was the old put-up-or-shut-up challenge, and he had me.

Within a few months, I was teaching workshops. Annoyance, rather than hurt, fueled me; anger gave me that extra little energy I needed to finally do what I'd been wanting to do. That, and the nudge from my roommate.

Comedian Al Franken took a break from writing political books for ten years after writing *Rush Limbaugh Is a Big Fat Idiot*. When asked about writing his next political tome, he professed to enjoy writing pure humor books more, but he had become so angry at right-wing commentators that he couldn't restrain himself from writing *Lies and the Lying Liars Who Tell Them: A Fair and Balanced Look at the Right*. Although Franken uses humor in this book, it is more pointed and not as funny as his other books. It's humor with a barb and a purpose, rather than just humor to entertain.

It is perhaps obvious that being upset about some issue can drive nonfiction. Barbara Ehrenreich (author of the popular books *Nickel and Dimed* and *Bait and Switch* among others) is clearly upset about income inequities and poverty

EXERCISE 2: DEFINING YOUR MOTIVATION

Write down why writing is important to you, and what you hope others will get from your writing. Then consider the following points:

- Are your reasons for writing are rooted in the past, present, or future?

- Does your motivation for writing have something to do with gaining something (like fame or money), or is it more oriented toward processing something (like a traumatic experience)?

- When it comes to your writing, are you more focused on the reactions of others, or are you writing purely for yourself?

- Now prioritize your reasons for writing. When your motivation for writing begins to flag, return to this list to replenish your natural motivational style by focusing your imagination or thoughts on the things that help energize you to take action.

- If you find your natural motivation style is hindering your writing, reprioritize your list and try experimenting with other styles to help get your writing going (e.g., try imagining something positive in the future if you have been past motivated; or try imagining how satisfying it is to find the right phrase or sentence to give expression to your nuanced experience rather than imagining others' responses to your writing).

in the world of work (she has also written about women's and class issues in other books). Michael Moore claims he hates to be a gadfly and is naturally shy, but his outrage has led to his documentaries (*Roger & Me*, *Bowling for Columbine* and *Fahrenheit 9/11*) and to his best-selling nonfiction books (*Stupid White Men* and others).

What annoys you in society or in other people? Can that issue become the theme for your next novel without making it too pedantic? Can it become the fuel that drives you through the process of creation and gives the book a focus? We've all seen movies that are boring because they so heavy-handedly try to make a political point. I find some of Michael Moore's movies a bit over the top and unfair, even when I am in sympathy with his basic point. Be careful not to let strong convictions replace art and good writing.

The idea is that you can use any form of energy—the positive, joyful energy or the angry, wounded energy—to drive your writing. Whatever the juice is for you, connect with it. I'll leave Ray Bradbury, a very energetic writer, with the last word on this:

> How long has it been since you wrote a story where your real love or your real hatred somehow got onto the paper? When was the last time you dared release a cherished prejudice so it slammed the page like a lightning bolt? What are the best things and the worst things in your life, and when are you going to get around to whispering or shouting them?

Motivational Patterns

We have learned a lot about the energies that motivate people. It's one thing to have energy, but another to tie that energy specifically to writing. The next step is to discover your particular motivational style. In my work as a therapist, I have discovered that there are different types of motivation, which can be grouped in three main categories:

TIME-ORIENTED MOTIVATION FOR CHANGE

There are three categories of time-oriented motivation for change—past, present, and future—and each can be categorized as positive or negative. Positive motivations involve going toward or wanting: joy, pleasure, desired consequences, etc. Negative motivations involve getting away from or avoiding: pain, fear, unwanted consequences, etc. I have provided some short examples to help you wrap your mind around each and identify which might be relevant for you.

POSITIVE

* *Positive Past Motivation*: John remembers the good comments he received from his English teachers in high school and college about his writing. This helps give him the confidence to write his first book.

* *Positive Present Motivation*: Mimi's friends love hearing her tell the stories about her pet dog, cat, and rat. They

urge her to write the stories down. She loves getting this positive feedback from her friends so much, she begins recording the stories.

- *Positive Future Motivation*: Every time her writing energy flags, Sarah imagines seeing her first book in print, giving it to friends, seeing a review in the paper.

NEGATIVE

- *Negative Past Motivation*: The kids in his school made fun of Ernie because he couldn't read. Remembering this humiliation makes Ernie vow that he'll show the world he isn't stupid by writing and publishing a book.

- *Negative Present Motivation*: Jan hates her job as a receptionist and wants to find another way to make a living. She begins writing during lunch hour and whenever she feels like skipping the writing time, she reminds herself how much she dislikes her job.

- *Negative Future Motivation*: Jack attends a self-help seminar in which the leader askes participants to imagine what will be written on their tombstones or said about them at their funerals. Jack realizes that his tombstone will read, "He made all his car payments on time and this realization depressed him." He makes plans to quit his job and finally write the novel he's been working on part time for the past few years.

INNER OR OUTER MOTIVATION

- *Internally generated and applied*: Having a good work ethic; setting small goals only you know about and keep; telling yourself you will only watch television after you have written a certain amount.

- *Externally imposed or applied*: Having a deadline imposed by someone else; signing a contract and getting an advance; promising someone else you will write a certain number of pages per day/week/month and then having them check to find out whether or not you kept your word.

I am very oriented to the future and what I want to have happen. In contrast, my wife is usually motivated to avoid a repeat of the painful past. These disparate motivations lead to radically different choices in life.

When you consider writing, how do you think of it? Do you imagine having the book in your hands and showing it to your admiring friends or family members? Or do you think of that third grade teacher who made fun of your bad spelling in front of the whole class? Do you think about how much fun you'll have just sitting and writing? Or do you remember all the effort you put into writing that story you wrote when you were a child and how proud your parents were when they read it? Each of these reflects a certain motivational style. If you find yourself focusing on the good things that will happen in the future when others are reading your book, you naturally use a future, positive, and external focus. If you think of the pleasure of writing and don't really care if others ever see your book, you probably have a more present, positive, internal motivational style.

"Author, know thyself." Find out what motivates you and use that to help you write, stick to your writing, and get your projects done. I heard a saying once: "It's easier to ride the horse in the direction it's going." Find out what direction your writing horse is already going and hop on.

COGNITIVE DISSONANCE: COMMITTING YOURSELF SO THAT NOT WRITING WOULD CAUSE DISCOMFORT

I have mentioned that one of my motivations for getting my books done—procrastinator and naturally lazy fellow that I am—was signing a contract with a publishing company, taking their money, and promising I would deliver the manuscript at a certain time. Promising myself would not have the power that promising someone else would have (especially when there is money and a legal contract involved).

So, think about yourself and what kind of commitment (public or private) could create what social psychologists call "cognitive dissonance," that conflict between what you say or believe and what you do. Would telling all your friends and family that you are writing a book do it for you? It wouldn't for me, but I have met enough other people for whom the shame of not following through after such public pronouncements was enough to get them off the dime and writing.

Would signing up for a writing course or writers' retreat be enough for you? Many people have used my writing workshops and retreats to finally get them to focus and follow through on writing their books. For some, they hate wasting money. For others, it is the time. For still others it is the social shame (their friends know they spent the money and the time to attend, or they feel an obligation not to let down the people they came to know during the course).

The bottom line is: What kind of action, statement, or commitment would it take to create enough friction between following through and not writing that you would very likely finish your book?

Fear as Blocked Energy and Fear as Clue

So now we know what the energy is and where it comes from. How about what blocks the energy? Fear—fear of success or failure, fear of being criticized, exposed, or known, and so on—can, if you give in to it, stop you in your writing tracks. Drawing upon the four energies above may be enough to overcome the fears, if the energy is stronger than the fear.

Stephen King used his worry about obsessed fans in one of his books, *Misery*. Instead of withdrawing from fear, as phobic people often do, King takes on the fear. He engages it through the writing, perhaps exorcising it or at least coming to terms with it. Thus writing can be a form of self-psychotherapy.

Ralph Keyes, in his book *The Courage to Write*, makes another point about fear and the energy to write. He suggests that whatever you are afraid to write is exactly what

28

you need to write. The juice is bound up in that area of fear. One way to get to this energy, then, is to search for what you are terrified of writing. Then write that. Another way to unearth this energy is to consider what you would write if you weren't afraid or if no one would read your writing. If you told the whole truth and nothing but the truth and wrote exactly what you feel you should write, what would that writing be?

FEAR OF REJECTION

I saw a cartoon a few years ago entitled "Really Brief Therapy." It showed a therapist's hand slapping a patient across the face, with the caption "Get over it."

That is my initial response when I hear people tell me they don't write or have stopped writing due to fear. There are many kinds of fear, of course, but here I will mostly speak of the fear of rejection, as that is one of the biggest obstacles.

You will almost certainly experience some rejection if you write, so get ready for it. Those lucky enough to get an agent or get published without being rejected first (a tiny minority, I'm sure you know) are sure to be dissed or criticized by someone sometime in their writing life. Garrison Keillor tells us that John Berryman used to say to writers, "You don't know if it's any good, and you never will know. And if you need to know, don't write." I wouldn't be so adamant about not writing, but he has a point. Even if millions like it, you may never really know if your writing is any good.

English novelist John Creasey received 763 rejection slips before publishing 564 books. Get over rejection. He did. I might have stopped after the first six hundred rejections, but Creasey was clearly psychotically optimistic, and look where it got him. I suspect you will succeed long before you hit 763 rejections, so, comparatively, it should be a breeze, right?

As for those other fears—fear of failure, fear of success, fear of stalkers, fear of having too much money (just joking—you're a writer, remember?), and so on—I have three antidotes:

Walk through the fear. I read a story once about a room with a thousand demons in it, all with the ability to take your worst fears and make them seem real to you. If you were able to walk through the room and come out the other side, you would have a happy life. Once you entered the room, however, you could only escape through the far door. The key to getting through without becoming paralyzed by fright was to remember that, no matter what you see or hear or fear, you must keep your feet moving. Because if you did that, you'd eventually find the exit from the room of fears. Translate this into writing land: Keep those fingers moving.

Don't believe what fear tells you; it wants to keep you small and stuck. As a therapist, I saw many people with phobias. After a while, I noticed a similar structure to the phobias. The person would become anxious or fearful and then would listen to the fear telling them, "If you stay away from these things or restrict yourself to these areas, you will be safe and you won't suffer from panic." Like invisible fences designed to keep dogs in an unfenced yard by shocking them when they reach the boundaries, fear shocked people into staying confined to a supposedly safe area. The only thing was: It never worked. That is, the reason people came to see me was that they were still having panic attacks, or anxiety, or had become dissatisfied with the restrictions in their lives. The ultimate cure, even better than antianxiety meds, was to have them challenge the boundaries of the fear and jump through the invisible fence so often that their electrified collars lost their charges. Go through the fear and get to the bigness inside you and in the world.

Look fear in the eye and it may lose its power. I had a client who was sexually abused as a child. I asked her how it had stopped and she said it had been sudden, and strange. The man who had been abusing her had taken her on his boat to perpetrate the abuse. It had always happened the same way: He would drive the boat out to an isolated place on the ocean, drop the anchor, and abuse her. One day when she was thirteen, she had caught his eye just as he turned around after dropping the anchor. She said that she suspected they had never made eye contact before, but this day she looked at him and silently communicated the message, "I know what you are doing and it is wrong. You know it's wrong, too." They locked eyes for what seemed like hours, although it was probably only a few minutes. Finally he broke the gaze by looking down. Without another word, he turned around, pulled up anchor, and drove her back to shore. He never abused her again. She told me she had been terrified of him until that day. After that, she was never afraid of him again. It was as if looking into the eyes of what she feared had made it lose its power.

It can work the same way with whatever you have feared in your writing life. Look at what you are afraid of. Look at it clearly and closely. Follow the fear all the way to the end. So what if you get rejected? What would really happen if your family disapproved? What if you got famous and everyone surreptitiously glanced at you while you were eating at a restaurant or wanted your autograph? Would it really be terrible or would you find a way to deal with it?

THEY NEED YOU AS A WRITER: A LITTLE MESSAGE OF HOPE AND ENERGY

One last point on energy. When I lead my book writing and publishing seminars, at some point I give participants a motivational lecture.

I teach workshops nationally and internationally. Every year, organizers of the three or four major conferences call me informally to ask who I think they should have at next year's conference. They know that I go to several of these conferences and that I am constantly searching for the new trends and best speakers. The organizers are in a bind. They want to bring back their best speakers, but those speakers tend to get more expensive and less available as their careers and reputations develop. Participants also want new blood or they get bored. So, these organizers must pepper their conferences with new presenters constantly.

It is a similar situation in the book publishing field. They need new beans for the publishing machine on a regular basis. How else are they going to discover the next Dan Brown? How else could they justify the existence of all these people in the publishing houses and literary agencies? Capitalism, for all its pitfalls, can work for you as a writer. Every year they need more revenues, more profits. That makes them more selective but also more eager to find good new talent.

When I send my agent a new writer (who is good, obviously), she thanks me for thinking of her. That is a different picture than one sometimes gets of the agent, editor, or publisher attitude. Yes, they are overwhelmed with unsolicited submissions. Yes, they are discerning as to whom they accept or encourage. But they are constantly looking for new writers and good books. So I hope that gives you some juice to keep going in your writing career.

Key Points

- In order to write and be motivated to write, you need juice or energy.

- There are four varieties of energy (blissed, blessed, pissed, and dissed); find which one, or more than one, fits for you and follow that energy to get yourself to write.

- There's nothing wrong with having negative energies that fuel your writing, as long as you can transmute those energies into creative endeavors—you might even heal an old hurt or slight through your writing.

- Different people are motivated in different ways— discover your personal motivational style (past-, present- or future-oriented; toward or away from; internal or external) and use it to get yourself to write and to keep yourself motivated.

- Create a situation of cognitive dissonance in which *not* writing would threaten your self-image or identity or would conflict with your values.

- Sometimes our energy is bound by fear; you can use that fear to help identify where your energy is stuck.

- You might need to write whatever it is you are terrified to write; that may be where the juice is for you.

CHAPTER

2

Writing Begets Writing

Bum glue and moving fingers will get your writing done.

It's amazing how long it takes to complete something you're not working on.

—R.D. CLYDE

When I first had the notion to write, I knew something about myself that might stop me. I have a tendency to procrastinate and to *think* about doing things rather than doing them. (If you saw me on the day before this book was due, you would know that what I say is true.) Since I was very committed to getting my ideas out in book form (if not actually committed to or excited about writing), I decided then and there that I would not spend my time reading books about writing, or going to writers conferences, or doing anything else that didn't involve actual writing.

35

I must tell you that this made the process of writing much more difficult and resulted in lots of bad writing, but at least I got my books written.

I think there's a lot to learn from books about writing—how to get yourself to write, write well, and sell your work. Writers conferences are good places to get a sense of the field, to meet others in writing and publishing, and, sometimes, to help sell your work. But for me, there were dangerous traps in those activities, and I knew I was likely to do them instead of writing. In fact, I was likely to do anything and everything instead of writing, so I had to guard against any of those things that I might convince myself were really about writing but didn't actually do anything to get my books written.

This leads to the principle of the Zen of Writing: The only way to write is to write. All the rest is commentary, procrastination, reasons you don't have time or can't write, and so on. All the rest is Not Writing.

Bryce Courtenay, Australian author of many books including *The Power of One*, put it this way when asked how he wrote so much: Bum glue. He sits his ass down and writes. Even if you write standing up or dictating, you get the point: *Do it*. Courtenay says that since he didn't start writing until he was in his fifties and he has so many books to write, he writes eight months of the year and works twelve hours a day, six days a week until he finishes the book he's working on.

Similarly, John McPhee is considered one of the pioneers of creative nonfiction, with more than thirty books and one hundred articles to his credit, but I heard that in his early writing days he tied the sash of his bathrobe to the chair to keep himself in the chair writing.

Dennis Palumbo has a principle that puts it another way: "Writing begets writing; not writing begets not writing." He recommends that if you don't know what to write about or you don't feel like writing, sit down and write about not knowing what to write about, or not feeling like writing. Inertia will tend to take you in the direction you are going. If you are writing, you tend to write more; if you are not writing, you tend not to write.

Sinclair Lewis was once talking to some students about being a writer. He asked them, "How many of you here are really serious about being writers?" Lots of hands went up. Lewis asked, "Well, why aren't you all home writing?" and walked out of the classroom. A dramatic example, but I think he made his point.

On that same theme, Ray Bradbury was once lecturing at a creative writing class and was asked for advice: "Mr. Bradbury, you are so productive. You've written many short stories, books, screenplays, and so on. How do you get in the mood to write? Sometimes I'm just not in the mood." Bradbury looked over his big, white bushy eyebrows at the student and replied, "Sit down and write, son. It will take care of all those moods you are having."

Joyce Carol Oates gives much the same advice: "One must be pitiless about this matter of 'mood.' In a sense, the writing will create the mood. ... I have forced myself to begin writing when I've been utterly exhausted, when I've felt my soul as thin as a playing card, when nothing seemed worth enduring for another five minutes ... and somehow the activity of writing changes everything."

Your task as a writer is to write. Imagine if you were a plumber and you went to the house of someone who had hired you to fix his pipes. Would you tell him that you are afraid of failure so you are not really ready to work yet? Or that you have "plumber's block" and don't really know how to proceed? Or would you wait for the house to be completely quiet, with no distractions? Or would you attend plumbers conference after plumbers conference and listen to people say what a cutthroat business plumbing has become, much more competitive than when they started as plumbers? Or read book after book about plumbing before you touched a pipe? Or would you sit for hours trying to work out a strategy for approaching the pipes in an optimum way? No, you would think about it a little and then dive right in, working out the problems as you go. You would get some training; most of it would be on the job.

Same thing with writing. Dive right in. There are sure to be some problems along the way, but you probably won't know what they are until you get to them. So get to them by writing.

And disregard your feelings. As a therapist, I love to say this. When it's time to write, don't get in touch with your feelings; don't go with your feelings. Your feelings will usually be telling you that you can't write or that you are too afraid or it's not the right time or some other such claptrap. So, thank those feelings for sharing and then tune them out. Get on with it. Don't wait for the Muse to visit.

Here's why I say this. When you are trying to decide what to do with your life, what direction to go, you really must pay attention to your heart, your soul, your guts, your intuition, your feelings. But once you know that writing is right for you, the next thing that emerges for most new writers is all the doubts and fears and slings and arrows of outrageous self-sabotage and procrastination. Perhaps it is fear of the new and unknown. But until you establish a routine or track record that silences the fears, you must learn to ignore or override these negative, unhelpful feelings. Since most of us are used to attending to and following our feelings, this may seem counterintuitive. But think back to any new feat or major task you have accomplished and I will bet you dollars to donuts that you have had to ignore feelings of laziness, fatigue, fear, avoidance, and self-doubt in order to get the job done.

Are you getting the point I am hammering in yet? Writers who complete projects *write*. Sure, they have rituals and tricks and struggles. But in the end, they write. They write no matter what else is going on within them or the world. And they keep writing until they complete something.

Walking the Marathon: Persistence Often Tops Talent and Inspiration

I had two strikes against my ever writing a book. One I mentioned in the introduction: I'm not a natural writer. Another was that I was pretty undisciplined. But I did have one thing

GET THE DAMN THING WRITTEN!

Get a Co-Author

James Patterson has co-written several of his thirty-four novels (there'll probably be more than thirty-four by the time you read this). He says he has more ideas than time to write them. Tom Clancy farms out the writing of some of his novels based on ideas and characters he has created.

To get myself motivated and to help me learn to write, I co-wrote many of my early books (I write solo these days). I found the dialogue better than staring at a blank screen, and I figured I would learn something from each of my co-authors about their writing styles and writing processes.

Sometimes my choice of co-author has been a disaster. I ended up doing most of the work and still sharing royalties and credit, or it turned out to be more work than it would have been if I had just written the book by myself. But other times, it's been a delight, both the process and the outcome. One co-author and I spent much of our co-writing time laughing. The book came out great and is still in print almost twenty years later. Still other times, the co-author's writing and contribution to the project was fine, but getting that person to do his part of the work was like pulling teeth.

That leads to a suggestion: Try a small project or a trial period of co-writing before you commit to a book or bigger project. Like any other relationship in life, co-authors can be heaven or hell.

> I have another co-author, with whom I have done four books, who is much better at details than I am. If I can't find a reference as the editing process comes to a close, I am likely to throw out the sentence or paragraph. He would search to the ends of the earth to find the missing reference. Which leads to another suggestion for finding and working with co-authors: Find one with complementary skills. If you are good with dialogue but not plotting, find someone with that strength. If you are good at outlining but terrible at details, find someone who has those skills.
>
> I wouldn't have nearly as many books out now if I hadn't had co-authors at a crucial period in my development as a writer. Consider this option to get your book written.

going for me: It drives me a bit crazy to waste effort, so if I begin a project, I like to see it through to fruition. Two strikes were not enough to put me out of the game, since my last swing—persistence—was a hit.

There are other elements to getting your book written, but this one—the willingness to keep writing and revising until the project is completed—is the most crucial.

Stephen King got discouraged and threw out the first few pages of a novel he was working on. His wife rescued it from the trash, wiped off the cigarette ashes, and urged him to stick with it. He did, and it resulted in his first major sale—the paperback rights for *Carrie* sold for $400,000. He later wrote in his book *On Writing*:

... the realization that stopping a piece of work just because it's hard, either emotionally or imaginatively, is a bad idea. Sometimes you have to go on when you don't feel like it, and sometimes you're doing good work when it feels like all you're managing is to shovel shit from a sitting position.

Persistence is required—persistence in writing, getting the book done, and getting published. Whining and complaining that you can't get published or that there is too much competition diverts energy from your main task.

Because I have the future orientation I discussed earlier, it is almost torture for me to go through the publication process. I am already on to my next project when back comes the previous project, awaiting revision. Boring! I already did that project. I'm done with it. Still, it has to be done, so I do it. Next comes either another revision from the publisher or the page proofs. Double boring! I'm really done with this project now, and I definitely do not want to see it again. It's getting in the way of new projects, or just having time with my friends and family. But it has to be done, so I get down to it. Then they have the nerve to send it to me once more in galley proofs for a final review. By then, the only way I can focus on the damn thing is to read it out loud (usually to my long-suffering wife). Finally, finally, it is done. Then some months later, I have to talk about it on television or radio or to a newspaper or magazine writer. I'm so done with that book by then. But I do the interviews. You get the picture.

I've often thought about which of the people I coach make it to the publication stage and which don't, and why. *If I had to choose one thing that separates the wheat from the chaff, it would be persistence.* It certainly isn't talent. I've coached some people with amazing talents who remain unpublished because they have not persisted.

Of course, writing ability is important (pretty crucial for fiction writers, actually), but alone it is not enough. Kurt Vonnegut said, "Talent is extremely common. What is rare is the willingness to endure the life of a writer. It is like making wallpaper by hand for the Sistine Chapel." If it turns out you don't have even the minimal talent required to get published, or the idea for your book sucks, you'll find out eventually, but don't decide that before you give it a good, long, persistent try. (And, perhaps, don't get too attached to a particular book idea—many writers failed to get their first several projects published and later decided that was a good thing—the books weren't right. Even I don't get every one of my projects accepted for publication.)

Beware "Freewriting"

Over the years of coaching people to write books and get them published, I have come across some who have been influenced by Natalie Goldberg's "free" or "wild mind" writing methods or Julia Cameron's "morning pages" practice. These are methods designed to get one's critical mind out of the way so that writing happens. I'm sure Goldberg and Cameron have had students who have written and gotten books published, but the people I have met who have learned and used this method often have reams of paper filled with this unstructured writing and no idea how to write a book.

I am not putting down "freewriting" in general. These writing exercises may help you start or practice writing. I do want to warn you, however, that freewriting is *process practice*, when what has ultimately produced books and articles for me is a *product process*. Process practice means writing just to write, enjoying the process of writing or writing to improve one's writing. Product process means writing to publish. My best writing practice comes when I am writing for a purpose. I write to complete a book, not just to write. I write to be published. I have a strong desire to communicate through the written word and have people read my books.

If writing process exercises help you get the writing flowing and make you a better writer, by all means do them. If, however, you find yourself filling endless pages without completing anything or getting anything out into the world, it's time to stop practicing and start producing. Practicing your writing by working on articles and books intended for publication, working under a deadline or a contract, having the knowledge that an editor, publisher, or unknown reader will be reading your work—all this focuses the mind and brings an intensity to your writing. Anything that takes you away from your main task (which, in my mind, is writing and publishing your book or article), is potentially distracting and time-wasting. I'm sorry if this seems too task-oriented, but it is key to how I have written so many books. While there is nothing philosophically wrong with writing for writing's sake, it is not the focus of this book.

Getting Ready, or Procrastinating and Avoiding?

Only you can tell how much preparation you need to do before writing. Some people need to do a fair amount of preparation work before they write, and this saves them an immense amount of time and effort later. They may prepare by creating a detailed outline, or doing research for years, or creating elaborate character "back stories" with histories and details that will never be used in the book. But some people use any and all of this preparation as an excuse to put off writing.

If you haven't yet produced much actual writing or been published, you should be skeptical of too much preparation. It is likely to be part of your avoidance or procrastination pattern.

Take an honest look at your preparation and planning process. Which parts are necessary and which reflect putting off writing?

We all have our own avoidance habits. For my first several books, I had to let my magazine subscriptions lapse for the duration of the writing project. If a magazine was in the house, it had an almost magnetic allure for me. I could avoid reading books, since they were clearly going to take up large chunks of time, but a little magazine, with bite-size articles? Surely that would be okay. The trouble is that I would pick one up and be gone for hours. Since I was working full time and raising four kids, there went my writing time.

I coached a friend through his block in completing his dissertation. I asked him what he was doing instead of working on the dissertation. He described his morning routine: Get up, pick up *The New York Times* sitting outside his apartment door, fix himself some coffee, and sit and read the paper. Then he'd go to his desk and begin working on his dissertation. An hour or so after sitting down to write—during which he usually did nothing because he was stuck—he would have to get ready for work. I told him he would have to give up *The New York Times* for the duration of his dissertation. As a true New Yorker, he was reluctant, but finally agreed. We also made some other arrangements (using the baby steps approach detailed in chapter 4) to have him do at least ten minutes of research and write one sentence every morning. Once he did those small tasks, momentum favored getting the dissertation done, rather than dreading and avoiding it, and he usually kept going. He had the dissertation done in a few months, and he was free to read *The New York Times* at his leisure the rest of his life. (Actually, once he was on a roll and unstuck, he probably could have gone back to reading it, but we were both concerned he would slip back into old habits.)

What is the magnet for your avoidance or procrastination? What do you do rather than write? It's time to take an honest inventory of your preferred or typical ways of not writing. No one but you really knows what belongs on this list, because you can always fool others (and sometimes yourself). So, without being unnecessarily harsh with yourself, honestly admit what you do to procrastinate. Then, when you notice yourself doing one or more of these things, you can instantly apply the magical antidote: *Start writing!*

In fact, you might even link these things to make them cues for writing: The next time you catch yourself at one of your "nonwriting habits," sit down and write for five minutes (or more). Thus you will begin to train yourself out of those nonwriting habits and into writing.

Identify Your Time-Wasters

Time-wasters are somewhat different from the avoidance strategies discussed above. These are things you may do regularly but that don't really enhance your life.

For example, for most of us, getting down on the floor and playing with our infant would not be a time-waster; spending hours on end filling in Sudoku puzzles or playing Tetris (I guess that reference shows my age) or *World of Warcraft* or *Second Life* (see, I can be hip and current) would. Perhaps it is reading two newspapers each day or checking your e-mail every few minutes.

Early on in my psychotherapy career I learned hypnosis. One of the most interesting things about learning hypnosis was not actually using it in practice; it was discovering how much time in our everyday lives we spend in a trance. There's nothing wrong with going into trance. It can be quite enjoyable and an escape from everyday life. Why I bring it up here is that many of our time-wasters are actually our own trance-inducers. When we are in our "time-waster trances," we often lose track of time and are unaware of our commitments.

Take a minute to think about your favorite time-wasters. If you were to identify and scrupulously avoid only your top

EXERCISE 3: Identify Nonwriting Habits

Make a list of things you typically do other than write.

1. _____
_____
2. _____
_____
3. _____
_____
4. _____
_____
5. _____
_____
6. _____
_____
7. _____
_____
8. _____
_____
9. _____
_____
10. _____
_____

(Continue on a piece of paper if you need more room—and
God help you.)

time-waster for the next month, you could free up a good amount of writing time. I suggest you write down your most typical time-waster and decide on a length of time you will cease and desist from engaging in it. Start with a small commitment; say, one week or one month. Then put a sticky note in the typical place you indulge the time-waster. Or put it on your bathroom mirror, or all over the house, if necessary. Whatever works. Revisit it at the end of your chosen time and make a new commitment if need be.

Here's another suggestion you might find helpful and enlightening: Time your time-wasting activities. Whenever you begin one of your main time-wasters, set a timer. Turn it off when you have ended that activity. After a week, add up the time spent and you will see how much time you could have had for writing. (Get a friend or family member to time you if you find it hard to do yourself.)

Changing your time-wasting habits, at least while you are in your intense book-writing periods, can help break these trance states and keep you awake and aware enough to keep your writing commitments. Of course, writing itself can be a trance state as well, but at least it involves getting your writing done.

Having Too Much Time to Write

There is an old saying: If you want something done, give it to a busy person.

Most successful writers are very busy people and yet they get their writing done. Sometimes having too much time on your hands is the worst thing that can happen to your writing progress.

I met a friend at a conference a few years ago and when he saw me, he instantly launched into his latest update on the book he intended to write—one I had been discussing with him for years. He told me a friend had offered the use of his beautiful house in Spain for a month, so he could finally focus on getting his book written. I had an internal "oh no" reaction, knowing that he was unlikely to do much writing but not wanting to throw cold water on his hopes. When I saw him the next year, the book, of course, was no further along. I told him that experienced writers were able to use a month of isolation to turn out a book, but beginners would most likely be too daunted by all that blank paper—and too tempted by the exotic and interesting Spanish culture and landscape—to write, not to mention overwhelmed with the prospect of writing a whole book. Such a setting would be a boon to me now but would not have worked for me early on in my writing career.

So there you have it. When asked to give the most succinct answer as to how I've managed to complete over twenty books, I would say first that I just wrote until the books were finished, regardless of my fears, my flaws, my laziness, my procrastination, and other unhelpful feelings and thoughts. We have covered that in this chapter. Next I had a passion to communicate that helped pull me through the difficult and challenging writing moments. We covered that in chapter 1 about finding the juice to write. The third element that helped was that I almost always had a contract and due date for my books (and advance money) before I wrote the majority of the book, and that external structure was very motivating to me. We'll take up this third element in chapter 5 in what I call "The Promise Method."

Key Points

- The only way to write is to write; everything else (worrying, being afraid, procrastinating, and so on) is not writing.

- Persistence is as important as talent and inspiration.

- Beware of "freewriting" or similar techniques if they don't lead to completed or publishable projects; they may be your way of avoiding or procrastinating.

- Beware of overpreparation as a means of avoidance.

- Identify and challenge your time-wasters and procrastinating signs, and wake up from your "time-wasters" trance.

- Too much time to write can be as fatal for the new writer as not enough time.

CHAPTER

3

Do One Thing Different

Changing one small thing
to get your writing done.

You write by sitting down and writing. There's no particular time or place—you suit yourself, your nature.

—BERNARD MALAMUD

One of the approaches I used in my thirty years as a therapist was discovering and altering patterns to help people solve their mental health, behavioral, emotional, and relationship problems. Along the way I also picked up the idea of rituals, or "positive addictions." The idea is that you are going to have addictions, habits, and rituals anyway, so you might as well make them positive and helpful. Becoming addicted to running, for example, is better for you than cocaine.

A change in your behavior patterns and your rituals can also affect your life as a writer. Here's how.

Writing Patterns

There are two aspects of patterns I focus on: patterns that work and patterns that don't.

Human beings seem to develop patterns quite readily—we take the same route to work each day; we routinely wash certain parts of our bodies when we shower or bathe; we use our dominant hand when eating; we tend to have our arguments at particular times and places; and so on.

Developing patterns is usually helpful, or at least neutral. Patterns help us save time and be more efficient. But not in all cases. Sometimes we develop habits and patterns that worked in the past but no longer serve us well when circumstances have changed. Those patterns might even sabotage us.

My former father-in-law, Dr. Lofton Hudson, wrote twenty-one books. (He used to jokingly ask me whether, to fulfill some Oepidal urge, I had to write twenty-two books before I could stop.) He wrote his books longhand and had secretaries transcribe them into typewritten pages. He would then make corrections in the manuscript and have the secretaries retype the whole manuscript. When the computer came into use, the secretaries wanted to save themselves countless hours by putting the transcriptions into word processing files, where making corrections would be much faster and easier. Dr. Hudson, in his seventies at the time, did not trust computers and was adamantly opposed to this new plan. He insisted that they manually retype the manuscript. After doing two books this way, the secretaries found a computer font that matched the typewriter font Dr. Hudson was used to. They fed typewriter paper through the computer printer and he was none the wiser. They would finish his corrections in an afternoon but wait a week to submit them so as not to break the illusion. The point: Sometimes your writing patterns become so ingrained they can actually interfere with your writing progress.

Writer Elmore Leonard once remarked that he was keeping the only typewriter repairperson in his area in business. Far be it from me to give Elmore Leonard advice (I'd like to say I'd give my right arm to write like him, but I need it to write), but someday even that typewriter repair guy is going to die and there will be no more typewriter ribbons. Beware of using or holding onto patterns that no longer work. If you need the clacks and dings of the typewriter, find some propellerhead teenager who can program your computer keyboard to feel and sound like your old Corona or Royal and keep typing away.

In this chapter, then, I suggest you examine your writing patterns—discovering those that work and get you to write and complete projects, and changing those that don't.

Discovering What Works

The first element of this pattern approach involves discovering patterns that have been working for you. For this, I am inviting you to be like an anthropologist. Discover what the habits and patterns of successful writing are in your own life by completing Exercise 4 (on the next page). I have divided things up this way because some writers discover that different patterns work for different tasks.

EXERCISE 4: WHAT GETS WRITING DONE?

Like an anthropologist, by objectively observing and culling the patterns, you can discover what supports getting your writing done. Search in several areas:

What helps you get ideas or inspiration for writing?

_____

_____

_____

What motivates you to write?

_____

_____

_____

What helps you get your work organized or outlined?

_____

_____

What helps you write rather than not write?

_____

_____

_____

What is the best pattern for revisions?

_____

_____

What helps you complete projects?

_____

_____

_____

For example, I have found, through experimentation, that I outline best by putting pen to paper, but I write the body of the book best on a computer. Also, I get many of my ideas in one of two ways: while I am giving a workshop or when I wake in the middle of the night. I am usually a sound sleeper, but once in a while I wake up in the middle of the night with a very clear idea or outline for a new book project. My wife, hearing me slip out of bed, asks, "Where are you going?" "I'm having a book," I reply.

The usual elements I suggest people examine for patterns are:

* setting
* timing
* tools
* sound
* people
* sharing your work
* body position and movement
* mode of writing
* what parts of a project to work on first

SETTING

What surroundings are conducive to your writing, planning, or revising? What distracts you?

* specific pieces of furniture
* certain room or space, in your house or outside
* a view of the outdoors

- a special writing space or room
- isolation/solitude
- having other people around
- riding in a car, a boat, an airplane, a train, or on a bicycle

TIMING

Some people work best in the morning; others burn the midnight oil. Still others work whenever they have a spare minute. What time of day—and what time of the week, or season of the year—is best for you to:

- generate ideas
- outline or plot
- write
- revise

DURATION OF WRITING SESSIONS

Think about your ideal duration for a writing session. Now think about a realistic duration that fits with your current life and obligations. Does it work best for you to:

- work on your project every day, or leave it for a time and return to it

- work in short sessions (less than an hour), or longer sessions (several hours)

- use shorter sessions to do some writing tasks (research, revision, outlining, generating examples or character backgrounds, and so on), and longer sessions for writing

TOOLS

Tools are things like telephones, e-mail, or games. They can be helpful (maybe indispensible) but can also end up being time-wasters. Which tools:

- facilitate your writing process
- interfere or slow you down
- distract, or should be kept far away from you during your writing time

SOUND

When you write, do you prefer to hear:

- noise (white noise, television, family/household noises)
- music (rock, classical, blues, New Age)
- silence (shhhh!)

PEOPLE

Think about the people in your life. Who is:

- helpful to you in your writing process
- helpful in the editing process
- helpful in the idea or outlining process

- encouraging; lifts you up, won't let you sell yourself short or take the easy way out

- discouraging; puts you down or is profoundly unhelpful

- genuinely happy for your successes; helps celebrate your accomplishments with you

- envious or unsupportive; subtly—or not so subtly—undermines your writing life

- supportive; helps you stick with your writing when you feel like giving up

SHARING YOUR WORK

Is it important for you to:

- publicly commit to a project; share your work in progress at all stages

- nurture your work in private; let it come to gestation in a protected environment.

- share your idea or your outline and structure, but keep the writing to yourself until it is in good shape

- keep the idea to yourself, but share the writing with others at all stages

- share certain drafts (first draft or third draft) with others

BODY POSITION AND MOVEMENT

Is physical activity conducive to your writing process? Which of the following are most helpful for you in generating ideas, being productive, or getting over writer's block?

- walking
- stretching
- exercise
- hunkering down and not moving a lot

MODE OF WRITING

What mode of capturing your words works best for you?

- brainstorming or idea generation
- outlining
- writing
- revising, correcting, or editing
- speaking aloud and tape recording or having someone take down your words
- writing by hand
- typing on a typewriter or computer

POINTS OF ENTRY

What part of your project is best for you to work on when you are stuck?

- the ending
- the first line

- a story
- a character
- a title (book or chapter)
- the part about which you are clearest/most knowledgeable
- the part about which you are the most excited or confident

PATTERNS OF VIEWING AND DOING

For clarity's sake, I often divide patterns into two kinds: how you are viewing the situation and what you are focusing your attention on (this constitutes "the viewing"); and actions you take or interactions you have with others (this is "the doing").

Pay attention to ways you view your writing and what you do about and around your writing to discover these patterns. Most of the things I talk about in this chapter, and indeed, in the whole book, fall into these two categories.

Experimenting: Discover and Implement What Works (and Don't Get Stuck in What Doesn't)

Ralph Waldo Emerson said, "Do not be too timid and squeamish about your actions. All life is an experiment. The more experiments you make, the better." I concur. There is no one right way to write. You can model on others, emulate them, but you will ultimately have to work things out for yourself. The only way to know what works for you is to experiment.

GET THE DAMN THING WRITTEN!

Speak Your Book

In my early writing years, writing was difficult for me, but I was already giving two or three talks per month and had developed my confidence and abilities as a public speaker. Speaking was as easy as falling off a log.

Someone suggested that I begin recording my workshops and transcribing them to create books. I thought it was a good idea, and tried it for the first time with my book *Solution-Oriented Hypnosis*. I had someone record it, paid someone else to transcribe it, sat down to edit it—and discovered it was harder than writing a book from scratch. I found, to my chagrin, that I regularly spoke in ungrammatical sentences, skipped around between thoughts, didn't finish thoughts, and so on. It took me longer to finish that book than usual.

But the book was different, more lively, than all my other books. Readers who had attended my workshops said it vividly evoked my speaking style and was easy to read.

There was another strange result. I began to speak in more grammatical sentences and more coherently than I had previously. My writing and editing had affected my speaking.

I tried it again some years later with another book project and found it was much easier and went more smoothly. This time I didn't record a workshop. I just stood (I had to stand to get the energy and feeling right) in my office and recorded what I wanted to say. The book was completed a bit quicker than my usual writing projects and came out well.

So, if you are more glib and articulate when speaking, you might try this possibility to get your book written. With transcription software on computers becoming more accurate, you can even skip paying someone to transcribe it.

Bonus tip: Use a nice little digital recorder called a Roland Edirol R-09. It records with one touch, has a built-in microphone that has excellent sound quality, and the sound files transfer easily into your computer.

If what you are doing is working and you are churning out as many bestsellers as Frank McCourt, Stephen King, or Dean Koontz, stick with your patterns. If you are not happy with something in your writing, or you are not writing as much as you would like, start messing around with your writing patterns and habits. Begin experimenting with:

- different environments
- different time frames
- different interactions with people around your writing
- different tools
- different styles and methods

Do one different thing, or do one thing differently. You might make radical changes. You could use your creative imagination and try some bizarre stuff (write in the nude under your bed with a flashlight; write with a magic marker or crayon) or model on what works for someone else (try the bathtub or hop on a night boat if there's one nearby—what the heck?). Or you might try making small changes in patterns that aren't working for your writing, and gradually change your habits.

Let me give you an example. A person I was coaching did his best writing in the evenings. As he began to get older, he discovered that he could no longer stay up as readily as he had in the past. He began to fall farther and farther behind in his writing goals. But he was not a morning person and always got up at the last possible minute to get ready for his day. Together we made a plan to have him begin getting up one minute earlier each day. He hardly noticed that difference. By the end of the week, he was getting up seven minutes earlier. By the end of the month, he was getting up half an hour earlier and was using that extra time to write.

I once heard a well-known therapist remark that it was easier to teach people his radically new approach to change if they weren't already therapists, because he had to spend so much time getting therapists to give up their previous bad habits. I think this is true with writers, even successful ones. Do as much experimentation as you can early in your writing career, because many of your habits will stick and it will be hard to break them later. They say the only difference between a rut and a grave is the dimensions—some of us have pretty deep writing ruts that might kill our writing careers (or at least put them in a coma).

What writing habits have you developed that slow you down or don't serve your writing? What is one small thing you could do to begin to challenge or change those unhelpful habits?

64

Rituals

One of the ways to do one thing different is, little by little, to create writing rituals until they become habits that support your writing automatically. As I said at the beginning of this chapter, writing rituals are a type of positive addiction. They can help you keep writing or get writing.

There was some research done years ago studying children who were surprisingly resilient in the face of difficult circumstances. The researchers studied kids who had one or both parents who were drug or alcohol addicted. These kids were often neglected and traumatized, and usually had unstable home environments. Many of them, as you might suspect, grew up to have multiple problems: crime, drug or alcohol problems, depression, and so on. But some did surprisingly well. The researchers discovered that the kids who did better often had rituals that gave them some sort of stability in the midst of the chaos of their lives: Grandmother read them a story once a week; they went to the Boys' Club every day after school; dinnertime was always the same time and they sat at the same place at the table.

In the same way, rituals can help writers by providing stability amidst the stress of writing. Developing rituals can create a structure that helps writers get their writing done while dealing with the ups, downs, and challenges of the writing life. In this section, we will examine some areas in which you might develop rituals to help you get your writing done. (By rituals, in this context, I mean regular habits or patterns—there are other kinds of rituals, but we won't be dealing with those here.) While in the previous section of this chapter I wrote about changing things to help you get your writing going and completed, here I am suggesting doing the same thing over and over to develop a ritualized habit to help you write. As with other suggestions in this book, feel free to pick and choose among these ideas.

Neurologist and author Alice Flaherty (*The Midnight Disease: The Drive to Write, Writer's Block, and the Creative Brain*) thinks there is a neurological connection with rituals: "Habits are important. Hemingway wrote standing up. Your brain, through some kind of Pavlovian conditioning, is going to start getting on its little creative groove [when you develop wiring habits]."

INSPIRATION RITUALS

How do you get inspired? How do you find the topic or theme of your book? How do you get inspired to write? When you think about it, is there a pattern? If so, could you create a ritual to deliberately get inspired?

Some writers regularly read papers or watch the news for ideas or inspiration. I spend a lot of time in airports, since I travel to teach seminars several times a month, and sometimes I'm inspired by people I observe in the airport. I imagine their lives and their stories and make notes for my fiction projects from these imaginings and observations.

I also think about the most memorable people I have ever known—those who were charismatic, or especially annoying, or creepy (or both), and those with the most striking traits. These memorable characters become the basis for characters in my stories. Sometimes I mix and match people, combining traits to create a new character.

I like long car rides. One thing I like about them is that my mind begins to wander after a few hundred miles, and song lyrics, symphonies, plots for short stories, poems, article ideas, and book ideas appear unbidden in my mind. I have learned to bring a tape recorder with me to make notes on these projects. When I am stuck with any part of a book, I can set my mind on that section and go for a long drive, which often creates a breakthrough to a new way of approaching the subject.

Writer Jacqueline Winspear was inspired to write a series of books (her Maisie Dobbs mysteries) when she had a vivid daydream, almost like a miniature movie, while stuck in traffic. So when you need inspiration or are stuck, you might develop a ritual of taking car rides—or get yourself into a traffic jam.

I often develop my topics from teaching workshops. Someone in the audience asks a question that sparks a response I have never articulated before. Or I hear myself say something new or innovative. I occasionally stop and write down the idea because I have found if I don't, it might be gone later. I even say to participants something like, "Give me a minute; I've just had an idea for a new book and want to write it down before I forget it." Participants have told me that they don't mind this and are even proud to have been part of seeding a new book.

I also talk out some ideas with my wife. Sometimes she doesn't have any new ideas, but I discover what I know, feel, and think by talking things through with her.

Another way I get inspired is by hearing or reading other people with whom I disagree. My book *Thriving Through Crisis* was inspired when I heard a psychologist on CNN. He was being interviewed on the one-year anniversary of the 9/11 attacks and made the statement, "These people will never get over this. They will suffer from post-traumatic stress disorder the rest of their lives." I knew that he was wrong, both from my personal experience and from my knowledge of the research as a psychotherapist. I wanted to reach through that TV screen and throttle that self-righteous, smug little bastard. Instead, I wrote a proposal and sent it off to my agent. I should have noted that psychologist's name and sent him a thank-you note (along with a copy of the research studies that showed him how wrong his categorical statement had been).

For this book, I did something I have never done for any of my previous books: I compiled market research from potential readers. I have an e-mail newsletter that I send out once a month (well, when I am not too busy; otherwise it comes out once every three or four months). I asked readers of the newsletter what stopped them from writing and what helped them write. I had gathered a lot of that information from people I have coached through the years, but I wanted to make sure I covered the topic thoroughly. Some of the responses from newsletter readers were inspiring; some are even included in the book.

EXERCISE 5: GENERATING IDEAS

Answer the following questions for a minimum of five minutes.

1. Write down as many words or phrases as you can that relate your topic.

_____

_____

_____

2. Arrange those words or phrases in some kind of logical order that makes sense to you.

_____

_____

_____

3. Make each of those words or phrases into a "declarative" sentence (a sentence that states a fact or makes an argument, usually ending in a period).

_____

_____

_____

4. Now turn each of those sentences into a question, or an "interrogatory" sentence (who, what, where, when, why, or how question).

_____

_____

_____

_____

I also listened to a lot of audio interviews with writers about their writing process (thank you, Barbara DeMarco-Barrett, for your wonderful podcast *Writers on Writing*, and Steve Bertrand, interviewer extraordinaire for Barnes & Noble's *Meet the Writers* podcasts). I listen to or read other people on my topic to find what I think in contrast to them or to get great quotations.

You'll find a method for generating ideas in Exercise 5 on the previous page. I use this with people I coach and most find it useful. Let me give you an example of the use of this technique and then explain why it works.

In outlining and writing this section, I could come up with a quick list of words or phrases and organize them into an order logical to me:

- rituals
- regularly repeated activities
- writing rituals
- preparation rituals
- publication rituals

I could then turn those phrases into declarative sentences in which I assert something I think about the subject:

- Rituals can be important for the writing life.
- Rituals are regularly repeated activities.
- Having writing rituals is important.
- Having preparation rituals can help you write better and more quickly.
- Having publication rituals is important.

Then I could turn each sentence into a question:

- Why are rituals important for the writing life?
- Who are some writers who have writing rituals?
- What are some examples of regularly repeated activities?
- How can writing rituals help the writer write better or more quickly?
- Why are publication rituals important?
- When should one use writing rituals?

This approach is effective because it seems to me that the human brain was designed for problem-solving, and questions naturally evoke our problem-solving impulses. Sitting and staring at a blank screen or piece of paper is daunting; a list of topics only slightly less so. But ask someone a question and, even if he knows little to nothing of the subject, he will often attempt an answer.

OUTLINE RITUALS

Here's a simple suggestion I use all the time for myself. If I were going to teach a presentation on this topic, what are the main points I would like to include? Then I organize them into an outline for the proposed talk and voilà—I have my book outline.

Or try telling your idea to someone else who has no knowledge of the subject but is an intelligent, good listener. Have her take notes on the main points she hears. Then go over it. If she has misunderstood, you haven't been clear. Go back and clarify.

Some writers use "mind maps," graphical representations of their projects, to organize them. Others outline longhand and linearly. Some take notes as they occur to them or as they research on note cards and then rearrange those cards in some logical order. Some focus every waking moment on plotting or organizing the book, even while they are busy with everyday tasks. What works for you?

PUBLICATION RITUALS

After publishing about ten books, I noticed that my friends and family were getting jaded when another one of my books was published: Oh, another book. That's nice.

I was busy so I didn't really attend to this shift at first, but I no longer had a book release party; I didn't even go out to dinner to celebrate. I just opened the package with the new book in it, showed it to my wife, and put it on the shelf with the others. The publication just slid into the routine of everyday life. After a few years, I realized this was a mistake and decided we should plan a book release party for my next book. That felt right.

Humans need celebrations to mark transitions and to help things stand out from everyday life. Most cultures spontaneously create rituals to help people celebrate transitions and accomplishments. Creating celebratory rituals to mark publishing transitions—like getting a contract for a book, winning an award, or recognizing publication dates—can help you leave the previous project behind and pleasantly anticipate future transitions.

This kind of ritual is somewhat different from the other rituals we have discussed in this chapter. Those rituals involved creating regularly repeated activities. This kind involves things that don't happen so regularly. In this case,

72

the ritual is designed to make the experience stand out, so the ritual usually involves going to some special place or doing some special thing. That's why getting dressed up and going to the best restaurant in town is often used for special occasions like birthdays and anniversaries. Think of this kind of ritual in that way.

What do you do to celebrate your writing accomplishments or publications? What kind of rituals do you have or could you create to mark any transition time during the writing or publishing process?

Key Points

- Identify the patterns you have around writing that don't work and begin to experiment with small changes until you find what works.

- Identify patterns that work around your writing and do more of those.

- Develop rituals to help structure and support your writing life.

Baby Steps, Baby Steps

The small-steps method for getting your writing done.

I'm writing a book. I've got the page numbers done.

—STEVEN WRIGHT

Many therapists related to the movie *What About Bob?* and laughed at the pop psychiatrist's prescriptive program: Baby Steps. Take small steps out of problems and into mental health. As silly as it sounded, many writers have successfully used the same strategy to get their writing done. A Chinese proverb makes the point: Enough shovels of earth—a mountain. Enough pails of water—a river.

This chapter will detail how to use the small-steps method to get started writing and to complete your project. I will detail four ways in which to do this: (1) breaking up the task into smaller pieces, (2) breaking up the task into small increments of time, (3) taking small actions, and (4) breaking the mental barrier.

Breaking Up the Task, Part I: Small Assignments

The title of Anne Lamott's writing book *Bird by Bird* derives from an anecdote she tells from her childhood. Her brother, having put off a school report on birds, was panicking because it was due the next day. When their father suggested the boy get started, he cried, "But how will I ever do it?"

"Bird by bird, buddy," was the father's calm reply.

For years I put off doing my taxes in a timely manner. I am naturally disorganized and dislike that kind of paperwork. Each year, though, my tax accountant would remind me that I was losing lots of deductions and paying more taxes due to this procrastination. Receipts would get lost, and my memory of what was what would fade with time. I would file for one extension, then another. I faced this issue with dread and mostly avoided thinking about it.

Finally one year I determined that, if I—a well-known therapist—could not solve this problem, I was not worth my salt. I knew very well what I would suggest to one of my clients: Break the task into manageable pieces. So I took my own advice. It was such an abhorrent task that all I could do at first was locate the piles that contained much of the material I would need to give to my preparer. I committed to spending just five minutes once a week going through the piles and organizing them into receipts, tax forms, income information, and so on. Sometimes I would do more than the allotted five minutes, but sometimes not. I gradually began to see light at the end of the tunnel and spent a whole afternoon once putting things into file folders. Once my taxes were done, I used the same categories to create folders for the next year. This resulted in much less disorganization and, therefore, less time spent hunting through piles. I began filing for only one extension. In recent years, I have become much more organized and typically file my taxes on time.

It can be the same with writing. The task seems so overwhelming to beginners that they sometimes avoid engaging in it. If you are in that category, try using the small-steps method. The first way to use it is to focus not on the whole task but the smallest piece of the task you can. Even John Steinbeck used this strategy. Here's what he said: "When I face the desolate impossibility of writing five hundred pages, a sick sense of failure falls on me, and I know I can never do it. Then gradually, I write one page and then another. One day's work is all I can permit myself to contemplate." Writer John Saul said something similar: "When I start a book, I always think it's patently absurd that I can write one. But I know I can write fifteen pages, and if I can write fifteen pages every day, eventually I will have five hundred of them." I actually have the confidence that I can write the whole book now that I have done a number of them, but at first I was in the same place as Saul and Steinbeck.

A co-author of one of my previous books, Sandy Beadle, wrote me this recently:

> I have been struggling with bookus interruptus for years. My next book got waylaid when the energy was still there, the energy went away, it has taken far too long, and I really lost focus. I know that there's nothing like a deadline to get me focused, so I asked someone in my seminar if I could send her a page or a chapter every week. She did not have to comment, or even read it—just catch it. That was eighty-three weeks ago, and I just mailed my seventy-ninth file to her. Sometimes it's just a paragraph, once it was a picture, sometimes it's a whole chapter. I recently told her I was going to arbitrarily call it finished when I got to one hundred items, so that is not far off.

How can you divide your project up into bite-sized chunks? Here's a possibility:

After you make an outline, make a more detailed outline—as detailed as you can make it—with ideas for anecdotes, quotations, exercises, scenes, plot points, which characters are in the scene, where it takes place, and so on. Then transfer each of those detailed points onto index cards that you can carry with you everywhere and write on. Keep them bundled with a rubber band in chapter or section order.

E.L. Doctorow described the process of writing a book in such small-steps terms: "It's like driving at night in the fog. You can only see as far as your headlights, but you can make the whole trip that way."

GET THE DAMN THING WRITTEN!

Blog Your Book

Blogs are popular and numerous. A blog, for those of you who don't know, is short for "weblog," and is a column or diary published on the Internet. The entries are usually short (less than a page) and can be posted as frequently as once a day or as infrequently as people have time for.

Julie Powell began a blog while working as a secretary in New York City. Each day for a year, she wrote about her experience of cooking every recipe from Julia Child's *Mastering the Art of French Cooking*. She began the blog because she was dissatisfied with her life and wasn't confident she would follow through on the project until she began to hear from readers who urged her on and gave her confidence. And she did hear—in the hundreds, then thousands. The resulting book, done in small pieces daily on her blog, was called *Julie and Julia: 365 Days, 524 Recipes, 1 Tiny Apartment Kitchen*. It was published by Little, Brown and, as of April 2006, had sold more than 100,000 copies.

The blog Baghdad Burning, written pseudonymously by an Iraqi woman in order to keep the author safe, was turned into a book and went on to win the Samuel Johnson prize in Britain, carrying with it an award of $53,000.

A blog by Jessica Cutler called *The Washingtonienne*, a juicy D.C. insider's online gossip column, was turned into a novel and published by Hyperion in 2005.

Blogs could be a nice way to get yourself to write, every day or once a week. Even if your entire blog wouldn't fit perfectly into a book, you could take pieces of the entries and use them to begin or create a book project. You would also get writing practice and, since blogs are so informal, you would probably lose that performance pressure felt by most when first writing. In addition, if you make a mistake, your readers are sure to let you know! They might even suggest new topics or a new slant on your topic.

Bonus tip: WordPress (www.wordpress.com) is a free blog service that's easy to use and set up. I set up a blog with them in five minutes. While I'm not a technophobe, I'm not that technically savvy either, so I was impressed. You could have a blog up and running at no cost today—what are you waiting for? Get blogging and get the damn book written, one small step at a time (you might even earn some ad money if you set it up right).

Bonus warning: Blogs can also be incredibly self-indulgent and become time-wasters, so be wary. Sometimes you can't tell at first whether it's a bane or boon for your writing, but if, after some months, you find you are doing nothing with your book and the blog itself isn't going to turn into a book, drop it or do less of it for a while and get cracking on productive writing.

Breaking Up the Task, Part II: Small Increments of Time

Big things can get done in small amounts of time. Writer Max Barry wrote two novels (*Company* and *Jennifer Government*) over his lunch hours working as a "cuddler" (someone who follows up after the sale is made by the star salespeople) at Hewlett-Packard. It took him several years but he finally made enough money writing that he could quit his job and begin writing full time.

The most common strategy to get yourself to write when you are not writing is to commit to small amounts of time. Five or fifteen minutes seem to be favorites of many writers. This does not mean that you will only write for five or fifteen minutes. It means you promise to write for at least five or fifteen minutes per day or per writing session. You can write more if you want. But you must write at least five or fifteen minutes. This usually taps into the principle we mentioned earlier: Writing begets writing and not writing begets not writing. If you can trick yourself into writing a little, that trickle often creates a bigger flow.

What is the minimal amount of time you are willing to commit to writing each day or week? What is a realistic small amount of writing (number of words or number of pages) you are willing to commit to writing each day or week?

Since the human mind often works better with a limited and achievable finish line, I recommend that you make limited time commitments as well. Decide you'll write every day for one month, or that you will write three times per week for two weeks. If it works for you and is producing the writing you want, you can recommit or commit to a longer time period.

An experiment: For the next week, sit down with a kitchen timer and write for five minutes without lifting your fingers from the keyboard or pen or pencil from the paper. Write on a particular part of your book that you have preselected. Everyone has five minutes in each day he could devote to this exercise, no matter how busy. Most people can write about 250 words in five minutes. That's about one page of a double-spaced manuscript. Do that every day for a year and you'll have a book. Doesn't that seem workable?

Breaking the Mental Barrier

One of the reasons the small-steps method can be so useful is that it makes big projects seem less daunting mentally and emotionally.

The first person to run a four-minute mile was Roger Bannister. When he was trying to break the four-minute mark, several others were close to accomplishing the feat as well. But none of them, try as they might, could do it. It was theorized that the human body was not capable of the task. Bannister came up with a new tack. Since he knew it was impossible to run a four-minute mile, he decided not to focus on that, but only on running one-sixteenth of a second faster in each of his competitions. He knew *that* was possible. And gradually he closed in on—and passed—the four-minute mile barrier. (Incidentally, after he broke the barrier, several other runners did so that same year.)

When my friend, psychologist Stephen Gilligan, was an adolescent, his father was an alcoholic. They would occasionally exchange harsh words, and the favorite put-down of Steve's father was, "Who the hell do you think you are?"

Many years later, his father sober and their relationship much improved, Steve discovered that he had internalized his father's put-down. As he sat down to write his first book, he was stopped by a voice that asked, "Who the hell do you think you are, that you could write a book?" The voice stopped Steve for some time until one day it occurred to him that if the question wasn't used as a put-down, it was actually a pretty useful question for self-exploration. "Who the hell do I think I am?" Steve began to wonder. This take on the question broke the mental barrier and Steve completed the first of several books he has written.

I often joke that the way I got my first writing published was that I slept with the editor. I was invited to edit a professional journal and I slipped a couple of articles into that issue. They weren't very good; it was the first writing I had done. But it helped me get over the "I've never been published so I'm not really a writer" barrier. I found all the subsequent writing I did less anxiety-provoking because I had already been published. I had overcome a certain mental barrier with a small accomplishment.

Is there a similar milestone or goalpost for you? What could you do to make it there?

Another thing I have found useful in helping people change their counterproductive views of writing is to discover where they are focusing their attention and have them shift that attention to something else.

For example, if you are focusing on the idea that you will never get published or get an agent, and that stops you from writing, shift your focus to writing for the pleasure of it or getting the words down on paper. If you are focused on how you are not as good a writer as John Irving and that stymies you, compare yourself to a writer you think is bad and still got published. If you are focused on getting all the words and ideas perfect and that paralyzes you, focus instead on the number of words you write each day.

A technique that we use in psychotherapy is called *externalizing*. This involves identifying unhelpful inner voices or ideas that mess up your writing or motivation to write and then beginning to consider them as external to you. That is, instead of thinking, "I really sabotage myself by telling myself I am not a good enough writer to get published," you think of that voice or idea as an external influence. Try saying, "Self-doubt is trying to convince me that I am not good enough." Or "Self-criticism is whispering unhelpful things into my ear today." This change can help you shift your relationship to those undermining voices and ideas and, at times, make it easier to challenge them. Do you believe 100 percent what self-doubt or self-criticism is telling you, or do you have other ideas or thoughts on the matter?

You can do this in a more artsy or physical way by writing those unhelpful thoughts or ideas on a piece of paper or drawing some representation of them and then burning, tearing up, burying, or otherwise disposing of them.

For example, if you feel you are having writer's block, write the words "Writer's Block" on a piece of paper, then burn that paper, and follow up by dropping it in the toilet and flushing it down.

Here's another variation on this idea. Carry a heavy rock around with you (in your purse, backpack, or briefcase) that represents your barriers, fears, or problems in your writing. Carry it for several days until you become really annoyed with the burden. Then—without getting caught—place the rock in the garden of someone who annoys you. Or, on a more positive note, throw the rock in a lake and enjoy watching your fears symbolically sink out of sight.

There is something in the human psyche that can actually use this method to purge unhelpful influences. Try it and find out for yourself. (There's much more to this method—if you want to find out more about it, try searching the Internet for the term *narrative therapy*.)

Developing an Identity as a Writer

When I meet with my therapy colleagues, they occasionally tell me about some method or idea they have that strikes me as truly original and that I think should be shared with the rest of the world. At these times, I am apt to look at these people and intone, "There's a book in that. You ought to write that up and turn it into a book." Most of the time, these people look at me like I am from Mars. They tell me they wouldn't know the first thing about writing or getting a book published and don't consider themselves writers. They can't even conceive of being writers.

I was certainly in that camp before I wrote my first book. I had never known anyone who had written a book and published it. I was clueless about how to proceed. But these days, I do think of myself as a writer.

That shift in identity took time. At first I thought of myself as "someone who had written books," not "a writer." Part of it was that I still did a lot of public speaking. But more than that, I kept thinking I would not be a writer until I developed writerly habits: writing every day from 8:00 A.M. to noon; wearing corduroy blazers with patches on the elbows; smoking a pipe and sipping bourbon while pounding at the typewriter keys. None of these things ever happened and yet I kept cranking out books. Eventually I began to list "writer" on my immigration and customs cards when returning from overseas—that was the first element in stepping into an identity as a writer. Next I began to say "I write books" when someone asked me what kind of work I did. That gradually shifted to "I'm a writer."

In contrast, I imagined myself as an international speaker long before I was one. I shared this goal with some of my professional friends and they nodded politely. A few years after I had mentioned this dream to a psychiatrist friend of mine, I called him to set up a lunch date. He suggested a day and I told him I wasn't available on that date because I was going to be in England during that time. "What are you going to do in England?" he asked.

"I'm teaching several workshops," I replied.

"Are you getting paid?"

"Yes, of course; I couldn't afford the trip if I weren't."

"I can't believe it," he said. "When you told me that you were going to be an international speaker, I thought you were delusional. But you are doing it. Good for you."

He was right. I had been delusional. It was a *folie a un* (if that is really a phrase). I was hallucinating a future in which I was a well-known international speaker and it was my individual fantasy. But, after lot of speeches and hard work, I had convinced the world of my delusion. I had become an international speaker. Now thousands of people share what was once just my made-up reality. It is now a *folie a mill*, I guess (another nonexistent phrase, I am sure). However, it didn't happen by some New Age magical affirmation process. I dreamed it and then worked my buns off to make that dream come true.

Some people know early on, from their childhood or adolescent years, that they are writers. In his essay, "Why I Write," George Orwell wrote, "From a very early age, perhaps the age of five or six, I knew that when I grew up I should be a writer. Between the ages of about seventeen and twenty-four I tried to abandon this idea, but I did so with the consciousness that I was outraging my true nature and that sooner or later I should have to settle down and write books."

Most people, however, are not so lucky or clear. They have to move toward thinking of themselves as writers or even considering the possibility they could be writers.

The point I am making here is that it really supports the process of writing—opens the possibilities of writing and completing books—if you begin to think of yourself as a writer. Elizabeth George says it this way: "I write because I was meant to write, I was called to write. I was told to write. I write because that's who I am."

One of my e-mail correspondents says she thinks of herself as "a thinker, not a writer." She has at times shared her thoughts and ideas with someone, only to later see them in print with the person taking credit. She gets annoyed when she sees them writing what she didn't, but still can't imagine herself as a writer. She is afraid no one will read what she writes. Contrast her self-image with that of Isaac Asimov, who once said: "If my doctor told me I had only six minutes to live, I wouldn't brood. I'd type a little faster." I might say good-bye to my family and friends, but I know what Asimov meant. I have more books in me than I have lifetimes to write them.

What else can you do to move into a sense of yourself as a writer? Get a mock-up of a book cover with your title and name on it? Get published in the local rag? Whatever it is, start doing those things and someday, hopefully in the near future, you'll live into the dream of being a writer.

As the song in the cult classic *The Rocky Horror Picture Show* goes: "Don't dream it, be it." (If you remember that movie and see the fishnet stockings as you read these words, it carbon dates you to approximately my age.) Dream it and live into the dream. Make the dream a reality. To do that takes action. That's what this whole book is about. *Don't just dream it, do it.*

Key Points

- Break your writing tasks into the smallest pieces you can to make them more doable.

- Break things into small increments of time, small pieces of action, and break the task up mentally.

- Determine the mental barriers in your writing life.

- Shift your focus of attention to things that facilitate, rather than block or discourage, your writing.

- Externalize the unhelpful voices and ideas that hamper your writing life and begin to shift your relationship to those voices and ideas.

- Think about how to make the writing blocks or barriers physical and then symbolically get rid of them.

- Begin to think differently about your writing if your previous way of thinking isn't helping you get your writing done.

- Develop an identity as a writer; do anything that helps you start to think of yourself as a writer and other people see you as a writer.

- As usual, the broken record in this book repeats the admonition: Sit down and write and you'll be a writer and begin to think of yourself as a writer.

5

The Promise Method

Using commitments to get your writing done.

Promises are like babies: easy to make, hard to deliver.

—UNKNOWN

Earlier, I mentioned using external motivation and cognitive dissonance as methods to get you writing. In this chapter, I want to go into more detail and emphasize one aspect of these motivational techniques. I finished many of my early books through a combination of factors, one of which was a passionate desire to communicate. Another was that a publisher paid me money and I promised to deliver a manuscript by a specified date.

If I had promised *myself* that I would complete a book by a certain date, I might have finished it—or I might not have.

Too many times I have promised myself I will exercise regularly/daily/three times a week and broken my vow as soon as I became busy or "didn't feel like it." I rarely break my promises to other people, however—especially when I have been paid and have signed a legal contract.

In this respect, nonfiction writers are in a better position than fiction writers. I only have to write a small section of my proposed book, along with a summary and some marketing plans, and I can sell the book before I have written it. Fiction writers usually have to write the whole thing to sell it.

Combined with my intense desire to get the book out and have people read it and be influenced, this contractual obligation and the expectation of the publisher was sufficient to get my early projects completed and out the door. I don't need the element of the contract as much anymore (I have written several books without a contract in recent years), but it does usually give me a clear timeline for delivering the manuscript, which helps get the project completed in a timely manner.

Even if you don't have a contract, you can use this method to help you get your writing done.

Promise Someone Else

One person who attended one of my writing and publishing boot camps said she was there because she had promised her mentor on his deathbed that she would finally write the book she had been hoping to write for many years. Another had promised his congregation publicly that he would write a book based on his most popular sermon. He didn't want to continue facing them week after week without having written his book. That kept him writing during the weekdays and also helped him say no to all the pulls on his time as a pastor.

It sometimes helps to have a coach or friend who helps keep you on track with your writing. Whom could you recruit to take you at your word for writing or finishing your book project? I am not talking about someone who will pile on the guilt if you don't write, but someone who believes in you and your book and will be ruthlessly loyal in helping you finish the book.

I have coached people for years on getting their writing done and have found some things that work and some traps to avoid in making promises.

First, since you are a writer, perhaps I don't need to convince you of the power of words in making promises. When making promises, be careful of the language you use, as it could make a crucial difference. Self-help gurus and therapists have pointed out that certain phrases can set you up to fail or weasel out of commitments. As Yoda in the Star Wars movies exhorts Luke Skywalker, "There is no try; only do."

Phrases to watch for:

- I'd like …
- I want to …
- Someday …
- When I get enough time …

GET THE DAMN THING WRITTEN!

Fool Yourself With a Fake Trip or Other Commitment

I went to a time management workshop years ago and heard a story about a guy who asked his secretary to schedule four fake trips for him per year. He traveled often and had noticed he was always very productive before he left on a trip. He would make those phone calls he had been putting off, finish projects he knew he would not be able to work on while on the road, and so on (this happened in the days before cell phones and portable computers).

Four times a year, she would tell him his trip was coming up, and he'd get a lot of work done. And then four times a year, she would tell him at the last minute that the trip he had scheduled for the next day was not going to happen. He had been so efficient and productive that he was able to do bigger projects with the time he now had open.

Can you use something similar in your writing life? Is there some way you could fool yourself or get someone else to fool you into being productive with your writing? An artificial deadline that you believe is real? A fake trip? A dinner you thought you were committed to go to but turns out to be a fiction your spouse created to give you an unexpected few hours unscheduled you can use to write?

At the end of my writing and publishing coaching groups, I have participants tell the group aloud what they intend to do and what they promise to do to get their books written and published. Some say slippery phrases that don't really indicate a true commitment: "I hope to have three chapters written by the end of the year," or "I want to develop a habit of writing every day." These, to my therapist ear, are almost always indications of books unlikely to be written, and I gently coach them to make more definitive statements.

So what is a promise? A promise is something *you say you'll do*—not think about doing, not just want to do, or hope to do. If you were getting married and said, "I *hope* to love, honor, and obey" or "I *want* to be faithful," it probably wouldn't go over well with your intended. Or if you said to a friend, "I hope to meet you for dinner Thursday," your friend would get the sense you are not committed to being there. A promise uses definitive words rather than waffling words or phrases: "I *will* have my proposal done by December 31, 2007," instead of "I *plan* to have my proposal done by December 31, 2007."

A promise is specific: "My book will be done by October 1, 2008," instead of "My book will be done sometime in the next year." And there are two things about which to be specific: specific actions or specific results. A specific action promise might be: "I commit to writing at least fifteen minutes a day, six days a week, for the next month." A specific result promise could be: "I agree to have two chapters completed by August 3 of this year."

Sometimes one has to be even more specific about phrases or words whose meanings might be ambiguous.

For example, in the last promise listed above above, what does the phrase "two chapters completed" mean? Does that mean first drafts? Or finished, polished chapters you would feel proud of sending to an agent or editor? Be specific and eliminate ambiguity in the words or phrases in your promise.

A way to make promises more effective can be writing them down and speaking them aloud to others. I tend to forget my promises. I'm good at keeping them if I write them down; if I don't, I might keep them or I might not. Making a public commitment seems important for some people; it evokes a sense of responsibility or shame that helps them keep the commitment. I grew up Catholic and felt guilty about so many things, I think I have burned out too many shame cells in my brain, so this public shame stuff doesn't move me as much as it could.

I do well with another person helping to keep me on track, though. I call this person my accountability partner. He agrees to hear my promises and work out some procedures, usually regular check-ins by phone, in person, or by e-mail, to help remind me of my promise and to coach me through the hard parts of the project.

My accountability partners don't use guilt, only encouraging reminders and brainstorming conversations when I have gotten off track or stuck. After so many books, I tend to be a self-starter (and finisher), but every once in a while I bring in someone else when a particular project is not moving along or I am unsure I will get it done in a timely manner.

EXERCISE 6: PROMISES & COMMITMENTS

List five promises about your writing. Be specific about actions, timing, and/or results.

1._____

_____

2._____

_____

3._____

_____

4._____

_____

5._____

_____

List five promises about getting published. Again, get specific about actions, timing, and/or results.

1._____

_____

2._____

_____

3._____

_____

4._____

_____

5._____

_____

Do you need an accountability partner? If so, whom will you contact and by when? What, specifically, will you ask them to do?

WRITING COMMITMENTS AND PUBLISHING COMMITMENTS

There are also two areas in which writers typically make commitments or promises: writing, and the process of getting that writing published. I have found that knowing my books will get published gives me much more energy to write, so for me the two are intertwined.

Writing commitments include anything that gets the book written: for example, sitting down in front of the computer at certain times, or for a certain amount of time.

Publishing commitments are about anything that involves selling the book or getting it published: sending off three query letters to agents in the next week, or hiring a freelance editor to polish your proposal by the end of the month.

Use Exercise 6 to identify your commitments.

Promise God or a Higher Power: Getting Motivated to Write by a Higher Calling

I don't mean to sound grandiose, but I feel my books were commissioned by God. I don't have enough confidence, ambition, or talent to write books on my own and wouldn't have written one book, let alone many, without having a sense that it was something I was brought to Earth to contribute.

I feel as if the books are not about me and they are not self-ish endeavors—they are what God wants and calls me to do. I wasn't a very good writer when I began, but I was willing to learn because I had this sense that I had a contribution to make. I deliberately sought out the most brutal editing I could get from friends and editors at publishing houses because I knew I wanted to be a better writer in order to make my contribution more effective. I never let my bruised feelings or ego get in the way of that goal.

I heard a story about two physicists, Leo Szilard and Hans Bethe, talking to one another. Szilard mentions to Bethe that he has begun keeping a diary. "Why?" asks Bethe.

"To record the facts of the universe for God," replies Szilard.

"Don't you think God already knows the facts of the universe, Leo?" Bethe asks.

"Yes, but not this version," replies Szilard.

And that, to me, is the point. I was meant to bring a unique voice and vision to the world through my writing. I may not be the best writer, but I have a unique contribution to make.

Some years ago, I was on *The Oprah Show* talking about my book *Do One Thing Different*. A few months later, I received an e-mail from a woman who had seen the show and subsequently read the book, asking if I could give recommend therapists in her area that could help her with drug addiction. She thought the philosophy and the method I detailed in the book would work better for her than traditional addiction treatment, since she had tried that and it hadn't worked. I gave her some names and got a thank-you.

About a year later, I heard from her again, and she told me her story. She had been a heroin addict in her young adult years, some twenty years ago. One day she had heard a street corner preacher and converted to Christianity, giving up drugs on the spot. She subsequently got a job as the church secretary and receptionist. Every once in a while, she would stand up in front of the congregation and tell the story about how finding Jesus had cured her addiction. Then, about a year before my appearance on *Oprah*, she had needed back surgery and was given pain medication postoperatively. She didn't think that would be a problem—her drug addiction was in the past. However, she soon found herself dependent on the pain medication. When the prescription ran out, she began to buy pain medication illegally on the street and, by the time she had contacted me, was up to seventeen pills a day. She was afraid to tell anyone in her church, because she didn't want to let them down and was concerned that she would be fired, since she handled money regularly.

She called the therapists I had recommended, but soon realized she was so in debt she couldn't afford therapy. She decided to read the book once more and put its principles into practice (as the title suggests, they involve changing one small thing that is within your power to change in order to make a bigger change). She started to shave a little off one pill each day. She continued to shave a little more off the pill each day until she got down to sixteen pills. She repeated this procedure until, after eight months, she had weaned herself off the pills altogether. When she wrote to

EXERCISE 7: YOUR PLAN OF ACTION

1. I agree to do this action or accomplish this result:

_____

_____

_____

_____

_____

2. By this date or with this frequency or amount until this date:

_____

3. The person/people who will help me keep on track and be accountable is/are:

_____

_____

_____

_____

_____

4. If I have a setback or don't keep my commitment, I plan to get back on track by:

_____

_____

_____

_____

_____

thank me after getting off the pills, I knew that I had been right: God had wanted me to write that book, if for no other reason than to help this one person.

I don't know about you, but books have saved my life at times. Reading them has given me a lifeline during rough patches, taken me away from painful life experiences, or given me hope. If you can remember this when you are writing, it can keep you going or motivate you to begin. Maybe somewhere, someone is waiting to read your words and it will be the very thing she needs to read at that moment.

If writing seems to you part of your purpose for being alive on this planet at this particular time, or a particular book seems as if you were meant to write it, perhaps the promise you can make is to God or a higher power. Or perhaps you have already made such a promise just by being born and having the experiences you have had. Some people believe that when they are born, they have already made a contract in this life about what they are meant to accomplish, learn, and contribute. Writing may be the expression of your calling here on Earth.

Can you make a commitment to God, your higher power, or humanity that you will write your book? What difference do you think your writing could make in the world and why might it be needed?

Contracts and Money Paid

To descend from the cosmic to the mundane: Signing contracts and getting a check in the mail, with the promise of future checks, is a great motivator for me to get my books written.

Book contracts have the benefit of having built-in deadlines for delivery of the manuscript. The publisher is counting on you to deliver the project on time because they have their printing schedule and publicity plans in place far ahead. This is a variation on the promise to a friend—only it's not a friend, and it's binding. It's a pressure that works for me. I was the guy in college who would be up all night studying the night before the exam, or finishing the term paper due the next day.

Though I'm a bit better these days, having a solid and unambiguous due date evokes action from me. I have heard stories of writers turning in manuscripts years late or not turning them in at all, but this is unthinkable to me. I accepted money, signed a contract, and made a legally binding promise. I don't make any promise lightly, especially a legally binding one. (Plus I, like most writers, have already spent the advance by the time the book is due and don't want to send it back!)

Okay, enough of my yabbering on. It's time to put your feet to the fire and get you to make some commitments. See Exercise 7 for a worksheet on making a promise. Fill it out if you are serious about getting your writing done.

Key Points

- Promise someone else that you will write or get something written.

- Get specific as to time, timing, actions, or results when you make this promise.

- Find a partner to help keep you on track and to keep you accountable with your writing promises.

- Promise God or a higher power that you will write or get something written.

- Connect with your higher purpose or calling or the contribution you have to make through your writing.

The Solution-Oriented Method

Revisiting what has worked to get your writing done.

A good resolution is like an old horse, which is often saddled but rarely ridden.

—MEXICAN PROVERB

I created an approach to therapy called solution-oriented therapy, in which we try to find what works in people's lives and apply that to the problem to solve it. This is sort of the opposite of the Woody Allen approach, which involves spending decades analyzing your problems and their source, hoping for mental health to result. There is research that indicates people are more creative when they focus on pleasant experiences rather than painful or upsetting ones. American author, journalist, and screenwriter Gene Fowler said, "Writing is easy; all you do is sit staring at a blank sheet of paper

103

until little drops of blood form on your forehead"—but this does not have to be the case. You can find strengths and resources and use those to make your writing life better and more successful.

We took up this idea of finding what works in one way in chapter 3 ("Do One Thing Different"), but here I will broaden the idea and give some new ways to put it into practice.

Drawing on Your Strengths

One simple way to discover what works is to think back on the times you have done anything well or succeeded at something. I call this *finding your contexts of competence*. In what settings are things relatively easy for you? In what contexts do you feel a sense of mastery, or at least competence? In what areas have you accomplished something difficult?

While working with one writer who was daunted by his task, I found out he was a dedicated golfer. I asked him what he had learned on the golf course that he could apply to writing. He thought for a minute and answered that he always did best when he cleared his mind of everything but golf. He didn't think about all the undone errands or problems at home or work; he just focused on being in the moment and hitting the ball. When I asked how he could apply that same skill to writing, he decided that he would slot out some time each week, as he did with golf, and borrow a friend's office to get some quiet, uninterrupted time where he could focus his attention only on writing.

Another aspiring writer had survived breast cancer. She had gotten through it by focusing on herself and her needs, instead of following her usual pattern of taking care of everyone else. As we discussed how she could use this hard-won knowledge to get her book written, she realized she was going to have to tell several friends she would not be available for the long talks they were used to having. Doing so would free up several hours each week for writing.

Are you getting the pattern? Choose an area in which you feel confident or successful, then think about how you developed that confidence, or how you operate in that environment. Or remember how you overcame the odds to achieve something. This is important. You have to mine these contexts for the skills, knowledge, or methods you use that work. Then consider how you might use or adapt the strategies to your writing (see Exercise 8).

BENCHMARKING: WHEN HAVE YOU WRITTEN EASILY OR WELL?

In this part of the solution method, you find your best and most effective moments. In business, they call this *benchmarking*. Find your most successful moments and model on those to develop better writing habits (see Exercise 9).

EXERCISE 8: IDENTIFY YOUR STRENGTHS

1. Write down some area in which you have succeeded, accomplished something, feel confident, or are competent.

_____

_____

_____

_____

2. Write down how you succeeded or gained confidence in that area. What methods, skills, attitudes, or strategies do you/did you use?

_____

_____

_____

_____

_____

_____

3. Brainstorm with others, or think it through yourself, about how you could transfer the skills, attitudes, knowledge, confidence, competence, or strategies from that area to any place in your writing life you might need it. Write down some ideas below.

_____

_____

_____

_____

_____

EXERCISE 9: BENCHMARKING

1. When have you ... succeeded at writing?

_____

_____

... written something you were very happy with, or of which you were particularly proud?

_____

_____

... felt confident about your writing?

_____

_____

2. Write down how you succeeded or did well in that writing situation. What methods, skills, attitudes, or strategies do you or did you use at that time? Was it in a particular setting?

_____

_____

_____

3. How can you transfer the skills, attitudes, knowledge, confidence, competence or strategies from that time to your current writing life? Brainstorm with others or think it through yourself.

_____

_____

_____

_____

Get Over Your Feelings

Another solution-oriented inquiry I use with writers is: Where in life have you or do you transcend your feelings and get yourself to do difficult things? You don't feel like writing? Use what you know in other areas of your life to find the resources and strategies to transcend that reluctance and write anyway. Those of you who are parents probably know the scenario of being utterly exhausted and then having to wake up during the night to take care of your child. That definitely involves transcending your feelings of the moment to do what is best.

You've probably also done this sometime in your work life. Have you ever done a task at work you weren't into or didn't feel you had the energy or motivation to do? You did it because you wanted to keep getting paid or you were too timid to say no.

My point is that you have developed the muscles of transcending your feelings of the moment to do something challenging. Use those muscles to do your writing when you don't feel like it or when you feel like doing something else that would be easier or more fun in the moment (see Exercise 10).

Patterns of Completing Projects

We discussed patterns that work and patterns that don't work earlier, but now I want to get more specific. When you have completed something, how have you done it: Worked on it straight through without stopping? Recruited friends to help

EXERCISE 10: GET OVER YOUR FEELINGS

1. Think about times when you haven't "gone with your feelings" in the moment and instead did something you didn't feel like doing but knew you needed to accomplish.

_____

_____

_____

_____

_____

2. How can you apply the same strategies the next time you don't feel like writing or are not inspired?

_____

_____

_____

_____

_____

3. Experiment with deliberately doing some difficult things to build your muscle so it is stronger the next time you need to write. What are some things you can do that don't directly involve writing but would strengthen your "willpower" muscle?

_____

_____

_____

_____

_____

_____

you? Done it one little step at a time? Drawn out a map of the project before you started? Gathered all the supplies you needed before starting? Done some of it, let it rest for a time, then gone back to it? Worked in the early morning hours, late at night, or during the weekend?

One person I coached in one of my writing groups expressed a concern that he wouldn't be able to complete a book. I knew he had once successfully built a backyard deck, so I asked him to describe how he had gone about that project. He told me that he had bought a book about building decks and read that first, so he had the "big picture." Then he went and talked to someone at the local building supply store and got some specific pointers. Next, he made a list of the supplies he needed and bought them all, so that when he had time, he would be able to begin immediately. His first free weekend, he began. He worked steadily all weekend, breaking only for short meals. By the end of the first weekend, he had enough of it done so it became self-reinforcing. He worked on it an hour or so each night after work and then finished it, with the help of a friend, the next weekend.

I suggested that he use the deck project as a template for getting his book done. He had already read a book or two about writing, and he was attending one of my writing coaching groups when we had the discussion, so he had already done the first two steps. What supplies did he need to be ready to begin the project when he had time? (A new laptop computer and a corner of his basement where he could write.) He also needed an outline (which he developed during the session, so that was another element down). He made a plan to start writing on his first unscheduled weekend, about a month from the time the group ended. He would enlist the help a friend who was a good editor when he was about halfway done with his proposal and sample chapters, and would work every free weekend and one hour per night until his proposal was done. Then he would use the same structure to complete the writing for his book. After going through this list, he said he knew he could write a book. It wasn't so daunting after all.

Another writer was great at arranging dinner parties at her house. There were lots of steps involved but she always pulled it off well. She dissected her strategies for organizing, planning, and giving dinner parties and she had her plan of attack for her book writing project.

See Exercise 11 for identifying your patterns to completing projects.

Patterns of Not Finishing

Just as there are patterns for finishing projects, there are patterns for not finishing. As the unofficial motto of Internet ad agency Agency.com states, "Figure out what sucks and then don't do that!" Our strategy here is similar. Figure out the patterns in your life that don't work and make sure you don't use those in your writing life.

What do you do when you *don't* finish things: Begin them and then get distracted? Start them when you know you have other things to do? Put them away in a place where you won't come across them readily or soon? See Exercise 12 to begin your brainstorm.

EXERCISE 11: PATTERNS FOR COMPLETION

1. Think of your patterns of finishing things and draw out the patterns from them. Write down every element or strategy you typically use. Use as many examples of finishing things you can. Combine the best of any or all of them.

_____

_____

_____

_____

_____

_____

_____

2. Make a plan to use the same strategies and structures to get your writing project done.

_____

_____

_____

_____

_____

_____

_____

_____

_____

_____

_____

WRITE IS A VERB

EXERCISE 12: AVOID NOT FINISHING

Write down the elements of your not finishing pattern below:

1._____
_____
_____

2._____
_____
_____

3._____
_____
_____

4._____
_____
_____

5._____
_____
_____

6._____
_____
_____

7._____
_____
_____

Now, remember: *Don't do that!* It sucks. Any time you find yourself doing any part of your not finishing pattern in relationship to your writing, go back to your competence, solution, or finishing patterns and instead do one thing in those patterns.

I have a friend who seems to specialize in incomplete projects. He has a half-finished bathroom, with the wallpaper stripped off but no new stuff, and the wallpaper has to wait on the plumbing work to be finished, and who knows when that will be done. He jumps around from passion to passion in his work and project to project in his personal life. Whenever I talk to him, I wait for the new, greatest thing of the week. He has a lot of passions and interests, and that's good; but he doesn't seem to have a strategy for finishing things and bringing them to a point that he can share them with others or enjoy their fruits.

Most of us have areas like this in our lives. If I were to ask you what makes your projects remain unfinished, what would you tell me? For me, it would involve one or more of several elements: (1) holding myself to impossible standards, (2) making the project very complicated, with multiple steps that need to be completed before much progress could be made or seen, (3) not writing it down, and (4) not having a deadline or schedule attached to it.

Modeling on Others

Recent discoveries about our brains show the existence of "mirror neurons" whose functions seem to be watching someone else and learning from what the other person is doing. Our brains appear to be firing off the same patterns that would be involved in doing something by just watching it.

You can use this ability to be a better or more motivated writer. The most effective way would be to watch a productive writer at work. But since Stephen King isn't going to let most of us into his writing space to learn directly, other methods will have to do for us. Look for opportunities to learn what accomplished writers do, straight from the author herself: This can be done through books, interviews, or articles; lectures or writers conferences; pre-recorded seminars; or televised or radio interviews, to name a few.

A writer doesn't have to be famous to be an excellent model for your writing. You might find a less well-known writer and model on him. Listen to him tell you about how he comes across an idea for writing and then hones it into a project. Watch him get ready to write. Watch him write.

I saw an interview with Ted Turner, founder of the CNN, on the occasion of CNN's tenth anniversary. Asked to look back at the beginnings of the endeavor, he flatly refused: "I don't look back," he told the interviewer. "I always look forward." I found that a good model. I have used that future-oriented strategy many times since in my writing life. I am always looking forward to my next book and getting excited about future projects and becoming a better writer.

Or you can use your imagination, another blessing with which humans are endowed. If you were a well-established or productive writer, how do you imagine you would go about the process? What kinds of things would you be thinking about or focusing your attention on? What kinds of attitudes do you think you would have?

Barring access to writers, you can model on any success-ful or accomplished person. Who gets things done or suc-ceeds at their endeavors? How do they do that? Again, what actions, attitudes, interactions, thoughts, focus of attention, and so on do they bring to their successful projects? Can you imitate or incorporate those strategies in your writing?

Envisioning a Future as a Published Author

Another strategy from solution-oriented therapy is to envision a future in which you have already written and published something or a future in which the barriers to your writing have been removed. Then work backwards from that preferred or better future to the present and let it pull you forward. For example, I had an acquaintance who, whenever she felt her energy or her commitment flag during her Ph.D. program, envisioned herself walking down the aisle to receive her diploma to the applause and cheers of friends and family. She got through her dissertation relatively smoothly and quickly using this method. (Now she makes me call her doctor every time I see her!)

Viktor Frankl, a Viennese psychiatrist imprisoned by the Nazis during World War II, kept himself going by imagining the book he would write about spirituality, meaning, and psychotherapy when he was free. While there was no guarantee he would get out of the camps alive, this vision kept him going and changed his outlook and how he spent his time. He wrote the bestseller *Man's Search for Meaning* on spare scraps of paper during his time in the camps—first Theresienstadt and later Auschwitz—and gave lectures to his fellow inmates on how to find meaning in these horrific experiences and how to keep hope alive.

EXERCISE 13: LETTER FROM YOUR FUTURE

Write your present self a letter from your future self. Incorporate the following points:

1. Identify your writing dreams that have been realized five years from now.

2. Tell yourself all the things you did to accomplish your dreams, including attitude changes (for example, you wrote every day for one year and finished your novel or nonfiction project; you sent off query letters to twenty literary agents; you finally got serious about your writing; you got to be a better writer—anything you can think of that would likely lead to success).

3. Tell yourself how others responded to these accomplishments.

4. Give yourself some sage and compassionate advice from the future.

During the next month, do at least one of the actions or attitude changes your future self told you you had made.

_____

_____

_____

_____

_____

_____

_____

_____

The idea I am suggesting is: If you can't find the resources or solutions in the present or past, they may reside in the future. Go get them and bring them back. Here is a simple exercise for doing so; after completing it, try Exercise 13.

HOW TO BACK INTO THE FUTURE

- Envision a successful, positive, or preferred future in regard to your writing life or project.

- Then imagine what you would need to do today, or in the next week or the next month, to make such a future more likely.

- Do at least one of those things in the next week or two.

Finding and Trusting Your Own Style

I can't tell you how many times I have read writing advice that tells writers not to worry about correcting mistakes like spelling errors while writing the initial drafts. Taking the time for accuracy is said to impede the free flow of writing. I have never followed this rule. I am physically disturbed by typos. I feel them in my body and they bother me, so I correct them as soon as I spot them. I am constantly going back during the first draft when my word processor shows me a typo or misspelling. My point? Forget anyone else's rules and what works for them, and discover and trust what works for you. There is no right way or rules for writing. Every writer needs to find and work her own way.

It is the same with your writing voice, or style. Until Hunter S. Thompson developed his engaging style of Gonzo journalism, injecting his paranoid, angry, drug-addled thoughts and experiences in the midst of his reporting, most people would have said that it wasn't appropriate and would never sell. It worked for him. As he was fond of declaring, "I hate to recommend drugs, sex, alcohol, violence, or insanity to anyone, but they've always worked for me." Similarly, what works for you would not necessarily work or be recommended for anyone else. I can recognize my favorite writers' styles without seeing their byline. They use the same words as everyone else but in a unique way.

e. e. cummings wrote, "To be nobody—but—yourself—in a world which is doing its best night and day to make you everybody else—means to fight the hardest battle any human being can fight and never stop fighting." That is the essence of style and voice. You need to fight to find and keep yours. It is what makes your writing alive and unique.

James Patterson was writing one of his many novels, *The Midnight Club*. His wife was ill at the time and he was pressed for time. He wrote a few short pages for every chapter, intending to go back to flesh them out. Upon reading them later, however, he discovered that it worked. He had found his voice and his style: lean and fast-paced. Critics sometimes fault him for this sparse style, but it works for him and for his millions of readers. He has discovered how to "leave out the parts that readers tend to skip," in the words of Elmore Leonard.

I used to try to write articles to be published in a popular psychotherapy magazine called *Psychotherapy Networker*. I knew the editor well. I taught at their annual conference for many years. Each time I sent a piece to be published, though, the editor—my friend Rich Simon—rejected it. Finally, determined to get in the magazine, I worked very hard on a piece, gave it to all my friends to tear it apart, edited it ten times, and then sent it along, letting Rich know how hard I had worked on it and how much I wanted it to be in his magazine. I waited several weeks and finally got the article back in the mail with a note in red felt pen at the top reading: "Where's the Bill O'Hanlon we have come to know and love at our conference every year? He's nowhere near this piece. Call me. Rich."

When we spoke on the phone, Rich told me that the piece was very clearly written but was missing a crucial element that would prevent him from publishing it—my voice. I asked him what that meant and his reply was enlightening: "Anybody could have written this piece, Bill." He told me that if he were reading a transcript of one of my spoken presentations he would recognize the style and know it was me right away. I speak quickly, use lots of stories, have a wickedly irreverent sense of humor, am a little sharp and teasing, and so on. This article had none of that. Good ideas, clearly written—but no voice. Rich had given me a clue about where to look for my voice and how to recognize it when it arrived. Which it ultimately did.

I mentioned earlier that having a contract and knowing the book will be published is a great motivator for me. I remember the first time I wrote a book without a contract. I woke up one night and had a great idea. I got up and wrote a rough outline. I happened to have some time off, so I began to write the book.

To my amazement, my fingers began flying over the keyboard so fast I could barely keep up. The writing was funny, irreverent, and lively—like I am in real life. My previous books had a little humor in them, but their main trait was clear, useful ideas—a bit more "straight" and serious. With this book, I had finally found my style. I finished the first draft in a week. I wasn't worried about whether it would be published, or what my agent or a publisher might think of it. Whether it ever got published was not as relevant as the floodgates of writing it opened (which is fortunate, because it was a short book and my agent and publishers decided it was too short to be anything but an e-book—I loved it just the way it was and didn't want to change it). Writing has been easier for me ever since.

It could be that how you think you "should" write is the very thing holding you back from writing as freely or as well as you could. Now, I am not suggesting that you have to take a light or irreverent tone in your writing. Just that you find your own style—which may be serious and academic. If you are trying to be Carl Hiaasen and you are really more serious, you are blocking that natural flow and energy you have by trying to write like someone else.

Can you remember a time when you felt you had found your style, your voice, or your method, even though it was "all wrong"? What were the unique elements or methods you used at that time? Can you recreate or enhance that in your writing life? Likewise, can you remember a time when you felt constrained because you were writing the way you thought someone else wanted you to write? Psychotherapists call this "shoulding on yourself." Move away from the domination of those "shoulds" and give yourself permission to write in your own style, with your own rules.

Key Points

- Draw on your strengths: Investigate what works for you in other contexts besides writing and transfer skills or strategies from those areas into your writing life.

- Think back on times when you have written something easily or well and discover what you can glean from those best writing moments to use in your current writing life.

- Discover your completion patterns—how you finish things—and do that in your writing.

- Discover your incompletion patterns—how you *don't* finish things—and don't do that in your writing.

- Model on anyone accomplished to find success or solution strategies for your writing—especially writers, but any accomplished or successful person.

- Envision a future in which you have written or been published.

- Discover and develop your unique writing style and voice— you'll know it when you find it, as things will not only feel right but the writing will usually come more easily.

- Challenge the "shoulds" or writing rules that you have somehow taken on; find the writing methods and voice that work for you.

Anything Worth Doing Is Worth Doing Poorly

Embracing mistakes, failure, and imperfection to get your writing done.

Looking back, I imagine I was always writing. Twaddle it was too. But far better to write twaddle, or anything, anything, than nothing at all.

—KATHERINE MANSFIELD

At a conference some years ago I came across two colleagues deep in conversation at the bar. When I approached, they said, "Get out of here, O'Hanlon, we're talking about why we can't get our first books written, and you've written fifteen already." I sat down anyway and asked them what the problem was. They said they had both been trained rigorously as psychologists in the scientist/practitioner model, which stressed that psychologists should know everything about their subject—all the prior research and all the literature—before writing anything. Laughing, I told them

123

I wouldn't have written any books if I had held myself to such standards.

Then I told them about a book I had written about the work of Milton Erickson. In that book, I had asserted that Dr. Erickson was the first therapist to focus on envisioning the future in psychotherapy. A few years after the book came out, I received an indignant letter from one of my readers upbraiding me for not knowing that Alfred Adler had been the first therapist to use the future in therapy. I wrote back and asked for the exact reference, and later mentioned this incident in a workshop. One of the participants told me that Carl Jung had actually been the first, and we both had it wrong. I asked for the reference again. So now, thanks to the power of community research, I have a complete picture of that small part of my book. (Although it wouldn't surprise me if someone reading this book offered yet another correction to this information.) If I had waited to get it all right before writing, I wouldn't have the book done and I probably wouldn't have found those details on my own anyway.

The point: Don't be a slacker and fail to do research or due diligence before you write; but don't paralyze yourself with undue perfectionism. I had read widely in the therapy field but because I didn't specialize in the work of Jung or Adler, I hadn't known of that aspect of their works.

Dive In

I used to work in a private psychotherapy clinic where we often had medical students coming in as interns to work with

GET THE DAMN THING WRITTEN!

Write Your Way Through a Crisis

If you are having a crisis in your life, consider taking the energy and pain from the crisis and putting it on the page. Write yourself through the crisis. Perhaps the material will be publishable or perhaps it will just help you transform your pain into something a bit more tolerable. Research shows that writing about a crisis, trauma, or painful event for as little as a few days can help the healing significantly.

Another way to use the crisis: Every time you feel upset, let it serve as a cue to work on your book project. It will give you something else to focus on instead of the misery and pain you are feeling, and something positive and tangible will emerge from this difficult time.

Your assignment then:

- Sit down and write about any traumatic or troubling event in your past, either recent or distant.

- Write as openly and honestly as you can without worrying about correct spelling or grammar or getting it exactly right.

- Write at the same time, for only fifteen minutes for three days in a row.

- Make sure you don't let anyone see the writing for at least a month.

This process can be useful for personal healing. Because crises can provide so much energy for writing, I am including it in this book, which is more focused on product rather than process writing. It can help you jump-start in your writing. As you continue to write, begin to shift your writing from purely expressive and personal to more communicative and universal.

clients under the supervision of more experienced therapists. One such intern was Audrey Berlin. Most of our previous students had been fearful of trying new methods in therapy, afraid they didn't yet know enough and would harm clients. Audrey was different. Almost from day one, she reported using the methods that we more experienced therapists were discussing in our clinical case meetings.

I began to observe Audrey. I noticed that she would hear or learn about a new approach and immediately use it in her next session, informing her clients that she had just come across this method and wasn't exactly competent at it yet, but were they willing to try it, as it might provide them with some help? Her clients knew she was a student and was learning as she went—they were getting their therapy free or at a substantial discount since they were seeing a student—and most readily agreed.

In contrast, at the beginning of my therapy career, I would hear about a new technique or theory, but decide I couldn't yet use it since I didn't know enough. I would buy books about the approach, attend more training sessions, think about the approach, talk about it with friends or colleagues—then decide I still didn't know enough. I'd buy more books, go to more training ... You get the point. For me, it would take months or even years before I got around to trying the new approach. Audrey tried it right away, and her progress was much faster than mine had been. I decided at that point to drop the "Bill O'Hanlon method" and to take up the "Audrey Berlin method."

I have found that it can be applied to areas outside of therapy—such as writing. The writing process involves both the creative, raw, get-the-words-down-on-the-page part and the painstaking, critical, editing, revision part. More writers stop at the raw part than at the editing part. It is in the raw part that you need to embrace failure, mistakes, missteps, wrong directions, being lost, stuck, clueless, and so on. "The fastest way to succeed is to double your failure rate," said Thomas Watson, Jr., longtime president of IBM.

But it is not enough just to fail. Recover. Learn something from it. "Whenever you fall, pick something up," said physician Oswald Avery. Said playwright Samuel Beckett: "Ever tried? Ever failed? No matter. Try again. Fail again. Fail better." Milton Erickson used to say, "If you fall on your face, at least you're heading in the right direction." American art instructor and artist Kimon Nicolaïdes warns students against avoiding mistakes, in his book *The Natural Way to Draw:*

Unfortunately, most students, whether through their own fault or the fault of their instructors, seem to be dreadfully afraid of making technical mistakes. You should understand that these mistakes are unavoidable. The sooner you make your first five thousand mistakes, the sooner you will be able to correct them.

They are all making the point that if you don't learn something and make adjustments, your mistakes and failures won't be as valuable.

I sent my early manuscripts out to my most literate friends asking them to tear the book apart as if they were my worst critics. They took me seriously, and my manuscripts were ripped to shreds. But I swallowed hard, took it all in, and ended up with not only better books but with a crash course in writing. (After twenty-plus books, I've burned out my literate friends for free editing, but luckily I am a much better first-draft writer and self-editor than those early days.)

In contrast, I also write songs. I have an entirely different stance about my songs. I consider them inspired and they come as a piece. I don't ask anyone to look at them or listen to them until they are in the final form. I rarely edit my songs and I certainly don't solicit criticism or editing from others. I also got perfectionistic about these songs, waiting years to send the songs out to people who could buy or record them because I want them to have the right arrangements and have them recorded on the proper quality equipment. It took me years to meet those standards. When I finally got them recorded and sent them out, a negative response would send me scurrying back into my artistic cave for a year or more, discouraged and licking my wounds.

Then the whole process of procrastination, perfectionism, avoidance, and isolation would recur.

In my mind, this explains why over twenty of my books have been bought and published and you have never heard any of my songs on the radio. Writing teacher Edith Ronald Mirrielees makes the point well: "As for the amateur, his difficulty is that his work, once on the page, hardens as cement hardens and can no more be changed. When he has learned to change it, to consider it in this light, to consider it in that, to hold the subject warm in his affections at the same time that his mind appraises the form—when that comes, he is no longer an amateur." I remain an amateur in the songwriting field but have become a professional in writing (a professional being someone who makes money at the endeavor as well as performing it to a certain standard)—all because I was willing to be an amateur, look foolish, not know, make mistakes, take corrections and feedback, and go out with my writing again and again.

If you've tried the (former) Bill O'Hanlon method and it hasn't worked for you, give the Audrey Berlin method a try. Go ahead and make mistakes, feel awkward, embarrass yourself, and so on. Dive in.

Writing Is Mostly Rewriting

I'm not the first to say it, but most writers find that after the initial burst of raw writing, much of the final product is the result of revision. I spend at least as much time revising as I do writing for my book projects. This goes back to the title of this chapter:

Be willing to write poorly just to get something on the page and then do a lot of rewriting. John Irving likens it to what he learned in being a wrestler. He had to practice the same moves over and over. From his memoir, *The Imaginary Girlfriend*:

> I have no doubt that I have learned more from wrestling than from creative writing classes; good writing means rewriting, and good wrestling is a matter of redoing— repetition without cease is obligatory, until the moves become second nature. I have never thought of myself as a "born" writer—any more than I think of myself as a "natural" athlete, or even a good one. What I am is a good rewriter; I never get anything right the first time—I just know how to revise and revise.

Some people not only accept the importance of revising, but embrace it with gusto. Playwright Nell Simon thinks it helps increase the odds of a writer's success: "In baseball you only get three swings and you're out. In rewriting, you get almost as many swings as you want, and you know, sooner or later, you'll hit the ball." Novelist Katherine Patterson revels in using the revision process to turn dross into gold or in her metaphor, "I love revision. Where else can spilled milk be turned into ice cream?"

This editing process is another reason it is so important to begin your writing projects with a great deal of passion for your subject. I made reference to this process earlier in the book, in chapter 1.

Key Points

- Give up perfection when you are starting out; be willing to make mistakes and write poorly.

- Do your research, but don't get paralyzed by the belief that you "don't know enough."

- Learn from your failures.

- Most writing is rewriting; embrace it.

- Don't get too attached to your words or your precious ego and pride; be loyal to the book instead.

It's Not About You, It's All About You

Taking the focus off yourself to overcome writer's block and other barriers to writing.

Write what matters. If you don't care about what you're writing, neither will your readers. So again you see: It's not about you and it's all about you.

—JUDY REEVES

In this chapter I am going to make two points that seem, as the title suggests, contradictory. But I don't think they are in conflict. I think of them as complementary. In one way, when you write, it should be an unselfish, un-self-concerned enterprise. In another way, your writing is all about you, coming from your deepest self and expressing yourself.

If there's one complaint I hear again and again from editors, agents, and publishers, it's that some authors are just narcissistic, self-absorbed, and entitled. They think only of themselves when writing and during the submission and

132

publishing process. It's me, me, me. As if the editors and agents are supposed to be dedicated to serving only that author, waiting by the phone, instantly editing and returning manuscripts, hand holding for hours, arranging rehab stints, and so on.

I have heard stories of authors giving excuse after excuse for not delivering their manuscripts on time and then being mystified about why the editor or publisher was unhappy with them. I've heard other stories about authors being abusive, or yelling at publishers to get them on *Oprah*. Me, me, me.

It's not all about you. Other people exist and have their own needs. Even agents and editors—but more important, readers. I've seen proposals and drafts of books that are filled with stories about *me, me, me*. Unless you orient the book to the readers' needs, it won't sell well. No one cares about you, you, you (unless you are famous). Make sure there is something in there for them. (Of course, I am making this point dramatically. As I said chapter 1, you have to care about what you are writing. So, in that sense, it is about you.)

It's Not About You: Discover Your Altruistic Motives for Writing

When I first began to give workshops and do public speaking, I was terrified. I was a very quiet, introverted person and didn't usually speak in front of more than one person at a time. But I had a sense it was my calling to give talks; I felt I had something really important to communicate to my audience, so I soldiered on despite my fear. I would get gastrointestinal symptoms (which I won't detail for you here) for days, sometimes weeks, before I gave a talk. Once on stage, I would still be nervous, especially at the beginning of the speech, but would become more calm and confident as the day went on. That fear lasted for a few years.

I coach people in public speaking as well as writing. For years, I told them my story and advised them that they would naturally be nervous at first, but that the fear would probably diminish as they gained more experience and confidence. A few years ago, though, I thought of something else. I have told this to people ever since and it has helped them quite a bit: *If you are nervous during a speech, your attention is in the wrong place.* If you are focused on your rapid heartbeat, you aren't paying attention to the audience. You are there to communicate effectively with them. What are you doing paying attention to yourself?

That is why I gradually became more comfortable, even in those early days in my public speaking life, as the day wore on. I began to focus more on the people there, and what they were getting out of the talk, than on myself. After a few years, as I gained more confidence and became a better speaker, I could focus right from the start on the audience, on their experience rather than mine. So every time I found myself feeling anxious, it became an automatic cue to shift my focus of attention.

I would say the same thing about the writing process. When writing, or thinking about writing, if you focus on yourself and your needs, you might have trouble or experience writer's block. Stephen King writes, "Writing isn't about making money, getting famous, getting a date, getting laid, or making friends. It is about enriching the lives of those who will read your work and enriching your own life as well." Maybe that's why he can write so prolifically—he's not thinking about his own needs so much when he is writing. He is enriching the lives of his readers.

Sometimes others find validation or kinship within our books. They feel they are not so alone, not so alien; they discover there are others in the world like them and they live for the day they can achieve escape velocity and seek out those other kindred souls. Christopher Isherwood, a gay writer, said, "If one writes about oneself, the real motive must be to give reassurance to other people." Writing about oneself may seem self-absorbed or narcissistic, but its real purpose is other-directed.

It's All About You: Care About What You Write

At times I have been tempted to write for money, or because someone else had a good idea that I thought I could write. It's always been a mistake. I lose energy somewhere along the line and, if I finish it at all, have to drag myself kicking and screaming to the finish line.

A few years ago, I signed on with a new agent. I had a specific book in mind, but as we talked about the project, she seized on one part of the proposal I had written, telling me she thought it would make an interesting book on its own and would be easier to sell. Swayed by her conviction and enthusiasm, I redid the proposal with the new focus, and it actually came out very well. I sent it off to the agent and she was delighted. However, between the time I had sent it to her and when she got back to me, I had gotten a little distance from the project. It became clear that, although it could be a great book and I knew how to write it, it wasn't really the book I wanted to write. It was the book *she* wanted me to write. I spoke to her about it and her disappointment was tangible over the phone. She told me that this project would probably sell more than my previous books, and indicated that if I didn't sign on for this project, we would part ways. Although she seemed like a fine agent and I was sorry to lose her, I chose not to do the book and have never regretted it. I knew myself well enough that I could imagine the lack of enthusiasm, even resentment, I would eventually feel slogging through the book and during the editing and marketing process. I was right to turn down the opportunity.

Anne Lamott says, "To be a good writer, you not only have to write a great deal, but you have to care." If you read Lamott's works, you will see clearly that she cares a great deal. And so should you.

Key Points

- One way to get writing is to connect with a motivation to help others or contribute to the world.

- Another way to get writing is to write about something you care deeply about.

Clueless in Publishing Land

Three crucial tips for getting published.

In writing, I have found that success breeds success. Once my first book was published, the next one was easier to write, in two ways: One, I knew I could finish a whole book; and two, I knew I could get a book published. So did potential publishers and agents. I had a bit of a track record and that gave publishers, editors, and agents more confidence that I could complete a project. Knowing I can get a book published gives me more confidence, energy, and motivation to write more books.

I started out essentially clueless about writing and publishing. I did not know anyone who had written or published a book and I didn't know how to navigate the maze of the publishing industry. I had to work it all out myself. Because I have spent a lot of time thinking about this topic, and I have a knack for making complex things simple and accessible, I can now coach people on how to get published. In this chapter, I will give you my hard-won wisdom, in hopes that this will encourage you to write more.

One important thing to remember is that, as I pointed out before, most authors are a bit self-centered when it comes to the publishing process. They only consider their own point of view: "This is a great book and it needs to be published," or "I want to be an author," or "I've worked hard on this book," or "Why do they make it so hard to get an agent or get published?"

Most successful people know that the ability to see things from another's point of view—whether customer, friend, or partner—is one of the main keys to success. In order to get published and make the whole procedure less frustrating for all concerned, you should take some time to imagine the agent's, editor's, or publisher's point of view so you can learn how to make it easy for them to say yes to your project.

A few years ago I visited the New York offices of one of my publishers. It was about a year before the book released and I was making publicity plans with my agent, my editor, and the publisher's head publicist. I asked very tentatively whether the publisher would mind if I hired my own outside publicist to supplement the work they would be doing on the book. I remember being so worried that this publicist would be upset by the suggestion that I almost didn't mention it. But to my surprise, everyone in the room immediately nodded their heads and responded enthusiastically. I hadn't known enough about their points of view on this subject to guess what their reaction might be. Now, after more books and more experience with people in publishing, I have a much better sense of their challenges, pet peeves, and interests. It would behoove you to learn as much as you can so you can see things through their lens as well.

THREE CRUCIAL TIPS

To make it simple, I have organized the tips into three *P*s with some subtopics:

1. Platform
2. Positioning
   - Particular slant
   - Problem
   - Promise
   - Prescription/program
   - Population
   - Compelling title and subtitle
3. Proposal

My, What a Big Platform You Have!

Platform is one of the buzzwords in the publishing industry. While it is not the only element in selling your book, it has become increasingly important.

A few years ago, my agent invited me to New York City to make the rounds of publishers who had shown some initial interest in my latest book. The scene at the publishing houses was almost always the same. My agent and I would be ushered into a meeting room with a large table and, one by one, several people from the publishing company—usually an editor, a senior editor, a marketing person, and a secretary—would wander in and take a seat. After getting settled with drinks and introductions, they all begin with a similar phrase: "The reason we wanted to meet with you, Bill, is because you have such a big platform." I would nod and try to look as if I understood. The discussion quickly moved on and I forgot the phrase. After several of these meetings, though, and hearing it again, I asked my agent what "platform" meant. She answered that it was publishing jargon for my reputation and credibility. I have since learned a bit more about the word, what it means, and more importantly, how you can use the concept to make it much more likely you will sell your book.

To understand the concept, think of a literal platform, a stage upon which you could stand. Imagine you are among a throng of wannabe authors, all hoping to get the attention of publishers who are going to walk into the room. Those publishers are looking for their next author, but with this large crowd milling about it is going to be a challenging task. If you were standing on a platform, however, you would be head and shoulders above the rest, and therefore easier to spot.

Your platform, then, is made up of anything that helps you stand out from the crowd by raising your visibility and marketability. The good news is that once you understand the elements that make up a platform and how important platform is to selling your book, you can begin to build or expand yours, thus making it more likely you will be able to sell your book to an agent, an editor, the bookstores, and ultimately, your readers.

Here are some common *planks* many authors have used to build their platforms (I will explain them further below):

- credibility
- marketing abilities
- marketing channels
- mass media presence
- media abilities and experience
- your track record in publishing
- celebrity
- your reputation
- unique topic or slant on topic
- borrowing platform planks from others

CREDIBILITY

Credibility consists of experience or education, or a combination of the two. How much of an expert are you on your book's topic or genre? If you are a top neurosurgeon, you can write with credibility on some topic within that specialty. If you have a successful series of thrillers, you are more likely to be able to sell your next thriller. You would also be likely to sell any book, but you already have credibility in the thriller genre.

I have a master's degree. If I had a Ph.D. or an M.D., I would have a bit more credibility. I have, however, published many professional articles in my field of expertise (psychotherapy) and am recognized as an expert in that field, so that gives me good credibility when I submit a book on that topic to publishers. The fact that this is my twenty-eighth book gives me credibility on the topic of this book. However, my agent has told me that selling a fiction book would be almost like starting all over, because I don't have credibility in that genre. Notice I wrote "almost like starting over," because I do have some writing platform and some publicity platform I could draw upon.

What if you don't have any professional degrees or established credibility in the topic area or genre in which you are writing? Don't despair, as this is only the first of many elements of platform. The more you have, the better, but any combination may be sufficient.

Make a list of the things (or copies of articles, tapes, and other materials) that support your credibility, both in general and specifically for the book you are trying to sell, and include that when you submit to the publisher or agent.

MARKETING ABILITIES

Before meeting with those New York publishers, I had sent along a videotape with several interviews I had done on TV shows and they had all taken the time to watch. When I met with them, they all spoke about how articulate and good I was with the media.

I had also listed previous marketing efforts I had made to support my earlier books. The publishers can use all the help they can get selling the book and getting the word out in the world. An author who is ready, willing, and able to help with marketing is a more desirable author.

I hired media coaches when I first began to do publicity for my books. Even though I regularly give talks and am pretty good at talking about my books, I can always use help focusing the message and learning to get it across more effectively. Publishers can see that I am interested in marketing and willing to work at it.

Can you show publishers and agents that you have marketing abilities and are willing and able to do marketing? Even if you have never been on mass media, can you get a friend to videotape you giving a short interview? Can you at least indicate that you know how important media and publicity are (some authors just assume that their job is done once they write the book)?

MARKETING CHANNELS

I include a list in my book proposals of all the marketing channels I will use to promote the book. For example, I have a Web site that gets thirty thousand hits per month and an e-mail newsletter that goes to more than four thousand people every month. I do several speaking engagements per month at which my books are sold. I have blogs and podcasts. If you don't have blogs, Web sites, or podcasts, develop some between now and the sale of the book. They are becoming easier and easier to do. I regularly appear on radio and have appeared on television, in magazines, and in newspapers. I have hired publicists to help get the word out about my work and my books. Determine which of these routes fits your budget, your skill set, and your social resources (friends and family who might have some experience, connections, or knowledge in any of these areas).

MASS MEDIA PRESENCE

Do you have your own TV or radio show or newspaper or magazine column? These are the jackpots in this category since mass media is a great platform from which to sell books.

But even if you don't have one of those, you can build a presence these days through having a well-visited Web site, popular blog, or a podcast. The Internet has made it possible for you to easily create and publish your own content and bypass the big media gatekeepers. So if you don't yet have a mass media presence, before you pitch your book to an agent or an editor, establish one. You can be a video star by posting a clever or informative video on YouTube.com. You can use these Internet tools for more exposure or for direct sales and marketing channels.

MEDIA ABILITIES AND EXPERIENCE

I discussed the importance of demonstrating marketing abilities. There are many ways to market, and one of the most effective ones is through the media. I have appeared on some big TV shows, including *Oprah* and *The Today Show*, and that helped sell the books I pitched after those appearances. The more media experiences and abilities you have, the bigger the platform.

Even if you don't have such appearances on your résumé, you can establish a little bit of platform by recording a pretend interview. Quality video equipment is so inexpensive these days, and amateur video editing on computers becoming so much higher quality, that you could easily record an interview to give publishers and agents a sense of how you would be on television. One person I coached created such a video and included it with her pitch for a professional book. The editor who received her package was so impressed he suggested she do the project as a trade book instead (one for the general public), which resulted in a higher advance and bigger publicity budget for the book.

YOUR TRACK RECORD IN PUBLISHING

This goes back to credibility and also speaks to reputation, but I thought I would separate it out here and write just a little more about it.

Have you ever published anything before? Even if it was years ago and even if it was in a small publication, it may help you establish a little platform by showing that you can write and get something published. Obviously, if you have had one or more books published, this helps establish platform. If those books sold well, all the better. And it doesn't have to be books. Any writing that you have done, for newsletters or an in-house Web site, journal articles, or newspaper columns, is relevant here.

CELEBRITY

Unless you fit in this category or are involved in a national story or scandal, this probably won't be one of the planks in your platform, but I thought I'd mention it to help you understand the concept. If you are Britney Spears or Monica Lewinsky, you can probably write a book on almost any topic and sell a sufficient number of copies to make it worth publishing because many people know your name. Most movie stars and politicians end up writing books to both trade on their notoriety and to enhance it. Most often, they don't even write their own books (they hire ghostwriters to do the heavy lifting), since it is enough to have their well-known name on the cover. The book does not even need to be that good, although it helps if it is (or if there is even juicy or controversial material included in it).

YOUR REPUTATION

This refers to many aspects of how you are known—your integrity, your personality, and your presence. Have you developed a reputation in your field, in society at large, or in the publishing industry? If you are difficult to work with, your reputation may precede you and make it harder to get a book contract, unless the rest of your platform makes the underlying economic proposition compelling.

If an editor, agent, or publisher were to ask colleagues what it's like to work with you, what would they hear?

I make a point of sending along comments from a publicist I worked with on an earlier project. She wrote me a little note after the publicity campaign ended saying that I was a "publicist's dream" to work with: always there when I said I would be, willing to do an interview on short notice, and the interviewers had loved having me on their shows.

I also let publishers know that I have turned my books in on time. I make myself easy to work with by cooperating in their processes and keeping my word. Since I am not famous, I am helping to establish my reputation with them.

UNIQUE TOPIC OR SLANT ON TOPIC

Obviously, having a great topic or a unique and compelling slant on your topic can add to your platform. Since I'll say more about this below, I'll just mention here that many wannabe authors I coach are convinced that their topic is so great and their take on it so unique that publishers will be falling all over themselves to obtain the book. In truth, this is rarely the case. But it has happened, and making your topic or slant compelling and unique can be another solid plank in your platform.

BORROWING PLATFORM PLANKS FROM OTHERS

You can also enlist the assistance of others, with bigger and better platforms than yours, to raise your platform. Blurbs, or endorsements, from well-known experts or other authors, is the typical way newer or lesser-known authors do this.

You can also link your platform to others by publishing books that are take-offs or commentaries on best-selling authors. The raft of *The Da Vinci Code* imitators, challengers, or commentators shows this tack. If you've ever seen a book whose cover reminds you of a bestseller at first glance, that is a publisher trying to hitch the new book's star to the previous bestseller.

Okay. To finish off this section about platform, let me tell you two stories. For several books, I had an agent I didn't like working with. I found her disrespectful and untrustworthy. So, after I appeared on *Oprah*, I saw my opportunity to get a new agent, one I would find more compatible. I thought agents would be beating down my door, since my last book had sold well as a result of being on *Oprah*. I did some quick agent research and sent out five queries, asking the agents if they would represent me. To my surprise, the response was lukewarm: Three never even responded, one said no, and one said to call her. I did and we weren't really a good fit. More than a little discouraged, I ended up staying with my agent for one more book. After more disappointing experiences with her, I became even more motivated to find a new agent, but by then I realized I didn't really understand how the publishing business worked.

Over the next few months, I bought and read almost every book out there on the process of getting published. I was sitting on the couch one day, on about book number forty, when I exclaimed to my wife, "I got it! I know how to get a new agent."

The next day, I prepared a packet with a query letter, a proposal for my next book, and a video of myself on various TV shows. I sent it overnight to an agent I had thoroughly researched and vetted through someone who knew a fair amount about agents. I received a call the next day from this agent (my current one—she's an angel) and she offered to represent me. She had been swayed by the packet and by a call to the editor for one of my previous books.

What made the difference and what was my eureka moment? I realized I had been thinking like an author when I pitched my books to publishers and agents. I thought that if I had a great idea, they would see the value of it and want to publish it. What I had gathered from reading all those books about publishing and getting agents was that, while the editors, publishers, and agents were certainly swayed by a compelling topic and idea, they also had to make a business and marketing case for the book, both to convince themselves and the publishing house it could make money, and to convince readers to buy it.

I now began to pitch my books with the business aspects (my platform) more articulated and spelled out and more up front, rather than as an afterthought. That not only helped me find a new agent but also sell subsequent books.

After I came to this realization, I remembered another puzzling experience from a few years prior. I had published the book *Do One Thing Different*—the one that was featured on *Oprah*—with HarperCollins. Some time after the book was published, my editor, Toni, wrote me an e-mail and suggested a follow-up project: *Do One Thing Different for Depression*.

EXERCISE 14: BUILD YOUR PLATFORM

What is a platform? It is the physical evidence of anything you have accomplished in your field, or related to your specific topic, and/or the accumulated evidence of your experience and ability to write books and sell them. It may also include how big and motivated your potential audience is. Here's how you start measuring and identifying your platform.

1. List all the public speaking you have done.

2. List quotes (blurbs) from well-known people who say good things about you, your work, or your workshop/book.

3. List any Web sites you have access to that could spread the word about you, your work, or your project. How many visitors do they receive every week or month?

4. List any Web sites that you maintain or regularly contribute to. How many visitors do these sites receive?

5. List any mailing lists you have compiled and how many names are on it (e-mail, snail mail).

6. List any newsletters in which you are regularly featured or that put in a special announcement about you.

7. List any conferences where you have presented or will present.

8. List any TV, radio shows, Web sites, or podcasts on which you have been featured or could be featured (based on your own connections).

9. Make copies of articles, videotapes, and audiotapes of media appearances or presentations.

10. Make copies of interviews you have given or any articles in which you've been quoted.

11. List all awards you have received.

12. List all of your good reviews.

13. List any advertising you've done (or other people have done) that features you or your work.

14. List all of your degrees, if relevant to the book topic.

15. Gather copies of books and articles you have written or in which you have been featured.

16. Gather statistics and evidence that there is a good-sized audience for your book idea or that there is a trend that would support the book.

17. List all publicity that you are willing or planning to do in support of your book.

Do as many activities and gather as much new evidence you can to broaden and raise your platform between now and the time you submit your next project. Consider the following:

- The first step I plan to take to expand on or add to my platform is ...

- I plan to take this step by ...

- Other steps I plan to take or material I need to gather ...

Having been depressed as a young adult, then later treating many people for depression as a psychotherapist, I had some radically different ideas for resolving it, so I was immediately attracted to the notion. As we corresponded about it, we both began to envision a series of these books: *Do One Thing Different for Anxiety; Do One Thing Different for Trauma;* and so on.

I worked up a proposal and got it to Toni. She called me a few days later and said her publishing committee had turned it down. They thought there were too many books on the subject already and that it wouldn't sell well enough to justify doing it. Both Toni and I were disappointed, but we let it go. But I was surprised that, since Toni was already an insider and it was her idea, it didn't fly.

In retrospect, I realize I had let Toni down. She could have sold it, I think, if I had known to make the business case better by spelling out my platform. I didn't really bother with it, since she was already sold on the book and I saw it as a mere formality. But even internally, she had to make a business case for the book. She had to sell her colleagues and they had to think about how the book would be sold. I never made that mistake again. I think long and hard about platform, expanding it when I can, and articulating and providing evidence for the one I already have.

So, think about how you can create, expand, and articulate your platform so you can get published and write even more (see Exercise 14).

Positioning

I'm lumping the next things that make the most difference in selling your book under the general category of "positioning." By this, I mean that your book has to occupy a unique position in the marketplace or it may not sell because it will appear like too may other books already out there.

Your book idea and/or approach must be unique. It must fill a hole in the market. You have to find a particular and compelling slant or angle on the subject, and show that there is a population not being served by the existing books out there who are also motivated to buy the book. You might have a tie-in with a news event or trend. You might have a different program or prescription from other books on the subject. In any case, you must stand out from the crowd.

This book is a good example of positioning. When first submitted, the publishers who saw it all passed because I hadn't positioned it correctly. I wanted to write a book called *The Publishing Coach* or *Clueless in Publishing Land* that would tell people how to get themselves to write, how to write quickly and well, and how to get published. It would cover everything from writing, motivation, good writing, getting an agent, getting published, and so on. It was too broad and there were many other books on the subject. I knew that (and so did my agent), but I was so hot on the topic I thought my platform and passion might carry me through. Alas, no. But F+W, who is publishing this book, came back with a more clear and narrow focus that used the strong points in my platform (psychotherapist for thirty-plus years; author of twenty-plus books). They suggested I write a book called *Write Is a Verb*, mainly focused on how to get people off the dime and get their books written. That positioning was different from most of the books out there. I was convinced that they were right. It was better positioning for the project. If the book does well enough, perhaps there will be demand for a broader book and I will write it, but the way to enter into publishing land is usually through the narrow gate.

When I coach people to write and sell their books, sometimes they worry that, when they send out their proposals or book ideas to agents or publishers, some unscrupulous agent or editor will steal their great book ideas. They ask me whether they should copyright their idea or get agents and editors to sign nondisclosure agreements. Not only are these moves obvious signs of an amateur, but they represent a fundamental misunderstanding of things. Here's what I tell them, and you, about this matter:

Most agents and editors won't steal your ideas—not only because the vast majority of them are ethical and honest people, but more to the point, *because they have no interest in your ideas.* You will have to do your utmost to get them to even look at your ideas. Ideas are a dime a dozen and they see thousands come across their desks each year. Unique ideas are more rare, but still not enough. A unique slant on an idea, a great presentation detailing that uniqueness, a great platform, and a kick-ass proposal will put you at the top of their submission pile.

How then do you make your idea more compelling and prove it is unique? You differentiate it from all the other

EXERCISE 15: FIND YOUR FOCUS

William Zinsser said, in his best-selling book *On Writing Well*, "Every writing project must be reduced before you start to write it." This exercise will help you do that.

How is my approach to this issue different from anything else I have seen or heard on the subject?

_____

_____

_____

_____

_____

Other books are for anyone with this issue. Mine is targeted more narrowly to [*women; people about to get divorced; Southerners; parents of autistic kids having trouble getting insurance reimbursement*]:

_____

_____

_____

_____

_____

No one else has my program/prescription, which is:

_____

_____

_____

_____

_____

My writing or content is unique because [*I use cartoons; I have done a study that no one else has*]:

_____
_____
_____
_____
_____

I know there are no books out there like mine because:

_____
_____
_____
_____
_____

What will surprise people about my book or my approach to this topic is:

_____
_____
_____
_____
_____

The shortest description I can give of my project:

_____
_____
_____
_____
_____

My book is a combination of these two well-known books or writing styles or content or well-known people, cultural or movie concepts—for example, Dr. Phil and Dr. Ruth; John Gray combined with Donald Trump; E.T. meets Sigmund Freud. Describe yours similarly:

_____ meets _____

_____ in _____

_____ for _____

In the tradition of _____ but _____

Reminiscent of _____ but _____

_____ with/without _____

If you could make a visual image of my book, it would look like:

My book is like [*a soothing balm on a painful sunburn; a map to a lost traveler*]:

_____

_____

_____

_____

_____

_____

_____

EXERCISE 16: BACK PANEL COPY

Write a brief description of what your book is about that would grab a potential reader:

_____

_____

_____

_____

_____

For nonfiction authors: What bullet points/promises/benefits would you put underneath that copy?

- _____

- _____

- _____

- _____

- _____

- _____

Write out a brief biographical statement about you that would also be relevant to readers and grab them in some way. This is essentially a brief "platform" statement.

_____

_____

_____

_____

_____

_____

_____

EXERCISE 17: IDENTIFY THE PROBLEM

The problem that my potential readers are concerned about is:

_____

_____

_____

_____

This is something my readers really want to have but they don't have or they don't know how to get it:

_____

_____

_____

_____

This is something my readers really want to avoid or get away from:

_____

_____

_____

_____

If my potential readers don't know they have this problem, here is my argument [*my statistics; my data*] that will convince them they have a problem and they need to read my book:

_____

_____

_____

_____

similar books and ideas by clearly thinking about and articulating several crucial areas. You might do a survey or research that makes discoveries that no one else has. I have a colleague in the psychotherapy field who has done research for twenty years and claims his research can predict with a high degree of accuracy which couples are going to divorce within the next five years and which will stay together. No one else has such research and that gives him a unique position for his books.

If I were to create a statement that captures the unique essence of this book, I might write something like: "This book, by the author of twenty-seven books written in twenty-five years, shows you how to get yourself to write and write quickly. It is like a kick in the pants for authors, providing motivational strategies to help them get their books written. Drawing not only on his writing skills, but on his thirty-plus years as a psychotherapist who helped people change hard-to-change things, you will learn how to use your own psychology, overcome your procrastination and bad habits, and finally get your writing projects done." One of the things that distinguishes me is that I have written so many books. Another is that I have been a psychotherapist. Very few writing books are by writers who have written so many books in such a short time; none that I know of is written by a psychotherapist with so many books out.

If you are writing a fiction book, then your writing will be one of the strongest differentiators in the area of uniqueness. Do you have a strong voice? Are your plots or characters compelling and engaging? Is your writing lyrical and mesmerizing? While other elements of platform and positioning are still important, in fiction, writing quality is key, so spend as much time as you can making sure the samples you send are the best possible. On the following pages, you'll find some exercises for thinking about the unique positioning for your book.

THE HIGH CONCEPT/THE ELEVATOR PITCH

The notion of high concept comes from Hollywood where people only have a short time to pitch their ideas. They have to communicate the nub of the idea and its uniqueness quickly, perhaps in the time it takes to ride in an elevator with a producer, director, big star, or financier. Coming up with your elevator pitch or the high concept not only helps you sell your book, but makes it easier to write, since it is now more clear to you as the author. Ask yourself: **The shortest description I can give of my project is ,..** Finish this exercise on the previous pages.

Practice high concept further by choosing one popular book you know fairly well and write the high concept statement for it.

PROBLEM

Every book—fiction or nonfiction—solves a problem for the reader. People buy and read books because they want to pass the time, live in other worlds or lives, learn how to do something, get out of pain, avoid problems, realize dreams

EXERCISE 18: YOUR PROMISE

What will readers know, or be able to do, or stop doing, or prevent, or recover from, after reading my book?

_____

_____

_____

_____

When they read this book, they will know or be able to or accomplish:

_____

_____

_____

_____

How will this book help readers?

_____

_____

_____

_____

Hint: The promise usually taps into negative motivations (help decrease or avoid something I don't like—anxiety, depression, a bad job; avoiding a divorce; avoiding getting my book rejected by publishers) or positive motivations (help me get something I want or more of something I want—wealth; peace; my ideal relationship; getting a book published).

and hopes, be inspired, and so on. These aspirations reflect problems. People are bored, or missing some crucial information or knowledge, or don't know how to cope with whatever challenging situation they are facing.

What problem does your book address? Is this a problem people will really be motivated enough to buy a book about?

Over the years, some of the people who have approached me have shown me book projects that tell their personal stories of abuse, difficulty, and ultimate triumph. Okay, I say, but what's in it for the reader? Most people do not care about your life unless you are famous or have a very unusual story (sadly, a difficult childhood or surviving a life-threatening disease no longer qualifies as unique).

So your first task in positioning your book is to specify what problem it addresses for the reader. Problems usually come in two varieties: (1) things people want to obtain or go toward and (2) things people want to avoid or get away from.

PROMISE

What follows logically from the problem, then, is to make sure your book promises to solve the problem for readers. What promise does your book make about offering a solution or relief from the problem you are addressing? After they read your book, what will they know or be able to do that they couldn't before? What *benefit* are you offering readers? (A benefit is something everyday readers would say they want even if they had no technical knowledge of the area about which you are writing.)

Your solutions, benefits or promises come in two varieties: (1) giving people something they want or (2) helping them avoid something they don't want.

Again, in my coaching, I have found that some people are so close to their material or project that they confuse the means of getting to the benefit with the actual benefit. For example, if you are writing a book about helping people have sufficient income for retirement, you might mistakenly think the promise of your book is to educate people about the many different options for retirement savings. This is what they call in sales and marketing a "feature" rather than a benefit. A reader might want to feel safe or secure about her retirement, or the reader might want to be able to stop working at age sixty-two. The reader doesn't much care about how you get her there; she just wants the outcome. So don't focus on the process, your inside knowledge or expertise, or the process of getting to the outcome when you are articulating the benefit for the reader. The promise would be "financial security" rather than "education about obtaining financial security." Keep it simple and keep it clear (see Exercise 18).

PRESCRIPTION/PROGRAM

This section applies to nonfiction only, and especially the type of book commonly called a "how-to," "advice," or "self-help" book. This genre is sometimes called "prescriptive nonfiction" because the author offers a particular method, program, or prescription for obtaining the benefit and solving the problem. This is one of the best ways for you to position your book as unique and different from any other on the topic, thereby making it an easier and more compelling sell for agents, publishers, and readers.

What do you have to offer that is a unique solution to the problem and delivery of the promise? This usually involves steps, strategies, methods, or stages, sometimes with a time element: The Ten-Step Model to Losing Ten Pounds; Twenty-One Days to a Better Marriage; The Research Evidence of the Five Ways to Predict Premaritally the Likelihood of Your Getting a Divorce.

Sometimes the method lends itself to an acronym. Try to keep these acronyms to three or four letters to make them easy to remember. For example, the F.I.R.M. method of resolving impotence (*F*ree yourself from performance pressures; *I*nvestigate and rule out possible medical causes; *R*edirect your attention to your partner and to pleasure rather than performance; Make it mutual so neither partner gets the blame but both are involved in the solution), or the A.C.T. program for overcoming procrastination, or the S.A.V.E. steps for getting out of debt in a year. Don't try to force it if it doesn't result in an acronym and be wary of being too cutesy (the F.I.R.M. method above is on thin ice in that regard).

If you create a unique enough program, you will be less likely to hear "I've seen this book before," "It's not unique enough," or "It's already been done"—among the more common reasons in the publishing field for turning a book down.

EXERCISE 19: YOUR TARGET AUDIENCE

My target audience is:

_____

_____

_____

I want to reach everyone who:

_____

_____

_____

_____

The people who really need my book are:

_____

_____

_____

_____

The people who will most want my book are:

_____

_____

_____

_____

The statistics I have gathered to indicate the size (or motivation) of the potential audience for my book are:

_____

_____

_____

_____

POPULATION

When I ask people I coach about who the potential readers are, they often tell me, "Everyone." My answer to that is: "How are you going to afford the marketing campaign?" Let's say we just limited it to the three hundred million or so people in the United States, and you decided to do a direct mail campaign to every person in the country to let them know your book is published. To reduce costs, you send a postcard. That'll cost you millions of dollars and no publisher would undertake such a marketing campaign. Even Bill Gates and Warren Buffett wouldn't spend that kind of money, because they are savvy enough businessmen to know they would almost certainly never make back their investment.

So, it is incumbent upon you to narrow down the market just a tad. Who is most likely to buy your book and what is your plan for letting them know the book is available? Who, specifically, would potentially (and realistically) buy your book? (See Exercise 19.)

Thinking this through will help focus the book and its tone, as well as later marketing. It will also help you sell the book to an agent or a publisher. Look for statistics (such as: "Nine million couples are on the verge of divorce as I write this," or "Six million books about getting published were sold in the United States last year alone, and books about publishing typically stay in print for nine years"), and use statistics to bolster your case for the existence, size, and motivation of your audience.

Think about publications and other media that these potential readers consume. Where do they spend time? How old are they? Are they male or female? Any specific ethnic group? Any particular income level or profession? What other books have they likely bought or read? The target audience you are looking for is going to be some sweet spot between "everyone" and "an audience so narrow that you'll only sell to the hundred people interested in the topic" (so if you are writing a book on "Variation on Tax Recording Methods in the Ukraine, 1845–1860," stick with academic publishers—and don't worry about getting an agent for that one, okay?).

A book for newly divorced women on getting your financial life on track is going to be an easier sell than a more general book on getting one's financial life in order because there are already so many books on the more general topic. Unless you have a platform that is so large you can do Shakespeare on it, narrow and focus your target population as much as you can to increase your odds of publishing success.

The Secret of Great Titles and Subtitles

Okay, here's a special bonus section for you. Remember I told you that I was clueless in publishing land when I started? Well, occasionally I would propose a title that I really liked and my editor or publisher or agent would shoot it down. Sometimes I would argue my case, but ultimately I decided that they were the experts and knew best, so I would take their advice.

For the book that ended up being called *Do One Thing Different*, my initial title was "Insanity Is Doing the Same

Thing Over and Over and Expecting Different Results." The publisher liked the idea for the book but told me after they bid on it that they would not use my title. "I like it," I protested. "I've used the line in workshops and it always gets a laugh and gets the point across quickly."

"You can't say it on television," they insisted. "It's too long."

"I talk fast."

"No, Bill, that won't be the title."

We tried out many titles, and none worked. Finally we were down to the wire when the editor-in-chief came up with the simple title that stuck.

After having similar struggles with several other books, I finally decided I would use one of the skills I picked up as a therapist—discovering patterns that work—to help me.

I found a Web site that lists every best-selling title in the United States from 1900 on and began looking for a pattern. I found it fairly quickly. Here it is (and I think this insight alone is worth the price of this book—I hope you agree).

Bestsellers, with very few exceptions, have one- to four-word titles. No more. Fiction is usually three words or less (and one of those words is often "The"). You can put a boatload of words in the subtitle or even have several subtitles, but titles are short and sweet. Easy to remember. Easy to ask for in bookstores. Easy to tell others about. I have a colleague and friend, Michele Weiner-Davis, who wrote a book called *Divorce Busting*. It's about preventing unnecessary divorce. The title says it all. Another one I saw said it all: *Die Rich*.

The list goes on and on. *Seabiscuit. Who Moved My Cheese? The Shining. Running With Scissors. The Horse Whisperer.*

EXERCISE 20: TITLE AND SUBTITLE

Write down three possible one- to four-word titles for your book:

_____ _____

___ _____

_____

_____

Now write down a subtitle that contains a statement of the problem and the promise (and perhaps your program):

_____

_____

_____

Developing Titles and Subtitles

Try a visual image (*The Lion in Winter, The Red Tent*):

_____ _____

___ _ _____

Try metaphors (*Sailing Through Your Dissertation; Chicken Soup for the Soul*):

_____

_____

Try variations on familiar phrases, poems, songs, books, or movie titles (*All The President's Men; Read My Hips; Immaculate Deception*):

_____

_____

Specify the audience for the book (*Finances for Newlyweds; Fitness for the Newly Retired*):

_____

_____

Try opposites (*Rich Dad, Poor Dad; The Positive Power of Negative Thinking*):

_____

_____

Try reversal of the usual expectations or received wisdom (*Die Poor; Everything Bad for You Is Good*):

_____

_____

Use a question (*Who Says Elephants Can't Dance?*):

_____

_____

Use repetition, rhyme, or puns (*Change Your Brain, Change Your Life*):

_____

_____

Use numbers (Four Ways to; Five Strategies; The Ten Steps):

_____

_____

Use time frames (in Fifteen Days or Less, in Six Months):

_____

_____

The One-Minute Manager. Die Broke. The Secret. The Christmas Box. The World Is Flat. The Tipping Point. Eats, Shoots, & Leaves. Freakonomics. Emotional Intelligence. Good to Great. The Purpose Driven Life.

This is my observation and conclusion, but it's easy enough to determine for yourself. Visit your local bookstore or an online bookstore like Amazon. See if my theory checks out. A good theory should be predictive and I am pretty confident that, even though I don't know what the bestsellers will be when this book is finally published, they will fit the pattern. Remember to look at bestsellers, though: There are many books published that don't fit the pattern, but they rarely make it to the best-seller list. (There are always exceptions like *Everything You Always Wanted to Know About Sex But Were Afraid to Ask*, but perhaps that was helped by the fact it had the word "sex" in the title. And if you're famous enough, you don't have to stick with this rule, though it will probably help.)

If you can get the problem, promise, and population into your title, great. Having it all in the title, though, is rare. If you can't, you can use the subtitle. For example: *Start Early: Seven Steps to Preventing Alzheimer's Starting in Your Fifties*; or, *Marriage 911: Five Emergency Steps to Take to Rescue Your Relationship When It's in Trouble*; or *Nine Months to Get Back in Shape After You've Had Your Baby*.

Fiction books rarely have subtitles, but they are sometimes used to convey a bit of the same information. One of my favorite fiction authors, Christopher Moore, often subtitles his novels (*You Suck: A Love Story; The Stupidest Angel: A*

Heartwarming Tale of Christmas Terror; Lamb: The Gospel According to Biff, Christ's Childhood Pal). You know you are getting a quirky humorous novel when you read the title and subtitle together.

My book *Do One Thing Different* had an original subtitle of *Uncommonly Simple Solutions to Life's Persistent Problems*. That was okay. It said something about the problem the book addressed (*life's persistent problems*) and it made a promise (*you will find simple solutions to those problems in this book*). It didn't have anything explicit about the population I was targeting but, implicitly, it was self-help readers. The program or prescription was implied in the title (*all you have to do is do one thing different*). When the paperback version came out a year later, my editor asked me if I wanted to try a new subtitle and, because I had been thinking about this stuff and coaching people, I had what I thought was a better subtitle. There were ten "keys to solution" in the book, so I suggested the subtitle: *Ten Simple Ways to Change Your Life*. We thought that was better and used it. My new agent commented, however, when she saw it, "Which is it, Bill? One thing different or ten things? It's confusing." I had never thought of that and, in retrospect, I agreed. If I had to do it all over again, I would use: *A Simple Way to Create Change in Your Life—Fast!*

All right. Now that you know the secret, it's time to work on your title. If you already have a one- to four-word title, great. If not, find one. Try it out on your friends, family, and co-workers. Find out what their response is and whether they remember it a week later. People regularly come up to me and tell me, "I really liked your book, *Do One Thing*

Right." Or "I read your book, *Change One Thing*." *Change One Thing* was actually a better title, I think, but *Do One Thing Right* has nothing to do with the book.

Find a title that sticks and is easy to remember (see Exercise 20). Then work on your subtitle. I recommend doing this before you write the book if you can. I would have changed the way I wrote *Do One Thing Different* if I had had that title (or even *Change One Thing*) early on.

Proposal

First let's tackle the whole purpose of proposals. These days, almost all nonfiction books written for the general public are sold through proposals. You don't have to (and probably shouldn't) write the whole book before it is bought by a publisher. Why? In part because people in publishing are so busy, they want a brief overview in order to make a decision quickly.

The proposal is also a kind of business/marketing plan for your book, showing agents, editors, and publishing committees that there is a potential market for your book and that you can help sell it to the audience.

When I did my first proposals for nonfiction books for the general public, I was often frustrated because I thought my time would have been better spent writing the book than writing about what I was going to write about. After several of these books were published, I began to realize that proposals were not only for the editors, agents, and publishing committees; they were also helpful to me.

The proposal forces me to prethink the organization and content of the book rather than doing it while I am writing the book, which makes writing the book much quicker.

The proposal also insures that you have examined the competition and found a unique angle for the topic of your book. If you haven't, the book is less likely to be acquired by a publisher or taken on by an agent. Your unique angle can help sell the book after it is published—if it is truly unique, the book buyer who wants that unique slant or concept will find it easier to choose your book instead of the rest.

ELEMENTS OF A GOOD PROPOSAL

Here, as succinctly as I can make it, are the typical elements included in a proposal for a nonfiction book. There is no actual required or standard form for proposals and you can be as creative as you like, but you should have a pretty good reason to deviate from the elements listed here.

1. Title page
2. Overview and summary of the book project
3. About the author
4. Manuscript specifications
5. Chapter summaries
6. Analysis of the market and the competition
7. Platform statement/marketing plan
8. Sample writing

Let's take each of these in turn.

1. Title page. This is a one-page cover for the proposal. I always start with the word *Proposal* in the upper left-hand corner of the cover page. Below that, centered, should be the title and subtitle, followed by the author's name. If you have an agent, put his name and contact information below the title and subtitle. If you don't have an agent, put your own name and contact information in this area.

2. Overview and summary of the book project. Try to keep this as short as possible: two pages (double-spaced), more if you have to, less if you can and still get the point across. Cover these major themes quickly and broadly (think big picture):

- What this project is: self-help, how-to, part-memoir, part educational

- Who you are and why you are the right person to write this book

- What the unique slant or angle of this book is, who the intended reader is (and how large that readership might be), and why the book is needed by those readers

- How you can help sell the book and get the word out about it

- Why you have sent it to this agent or editor, if relevant

3. About the author. A short biographical statement establishing your credibility, your credentials, your accomplishments, and your marketing channels. Keep it to a paragraph or two.

4. Manuscript specifications. Another short paragraph telling the agent/publisher how long (in word count or number of pages) the book will be; whether it will have illustrations and how those will be created or obtained; if any permission or fees will be necessary to use other people's material (hint: unless it is essential for the book or you will be willing to pay, the higher these costs, the more potential strikes against the project); and the expected time to deliver the manuscript (this is typically anywhere from nine to eighteen months; I usually say a year).

5. Chapter summaries. This is an expanded outline, with narrative summaries of what each chapter will contain. Again, this should be as short as possible while still getting the point across.

6. Analysis of the market and the competition. This section should contain any numbers you have about the size of the potential readership for the book. And it should list and speak to other books similar to yours: how yours is different and fills a different niche or need. I do this research by going on Amazon and reading the reviews of books. I also visit bookstores. In these discussions, don't just put down the other books; factually summarize them, and then show how yours is different. (Hint: Don't claim that your book is entirely unique and has no competition. This may make the agent or publisher nervous, since it may indicate there is not really a market for your book.)

7. Platform statement/marketing plan. As we discussed, platform is a jargon word in the publishing industry that basically means anything that helps you or your book stand out from the crowd. It includes your marketing channels, your marketing capabilities, your credibility, and the size of your potential readership. In this section, you are expanding on your biographical statement by providing as much evidence as possible that the book will sell and how you can help it sell.

8. Sample writing. This consists of samples from any chapter or chapters that will give the agent, editor, or publishing committee a sense of the style of the book and your writing abilities. It can be from anywhere in the book; for example, it doesn't have to be the first chapter. If there will be charts, quizzes, illustrations, summary boxes, or any other special formatting in the book, include sections in which these occur.

That's how to create a good proposal. Now let's talk about, as TV chef Emeril says, kicking it up a notch.

CREATING A KICK-ASS PROPOSAL

No typos. Have your spell checker and friends who are literate and know grammar and spelling go over and over it. While the proposal doesn't have to be perfect to sell, errors of this kind are a turnoff and could put you in the circular file.

Always double-space everything. This one drives me crazy sometimes because it seems such a waste of paper, but this is the form editors like to see, since they are used to editing and making comments on double-spaced manuscripts, I guess. Proposals have been kicked back to me by my agent when I have tried to sneak in a section that is single-spaced.

Include some supporting documents or media material to illustrate your platform: audiotaped excerpts of radio interviews; clips from television; and newspaper and magazine articles.

Don't skimp on quality. Print it on a good quality printer on standard white paper using a standard font like Times New Roman in twelve-point size.

The biggest thing that will make it kick-ass and more likely to sell is having a unique slant on a topic that has a good audience and a good platform statement and evidence to back it up.

THINGS THAT ARE LIKELY TO LOSE YOU THE SALE

- Not having a unique and focused approach to your topic.

- Not having good platform material. These days, editors and agents need to make a business case for the book no matter how great the idea or writing may be.

- Bragging or making grandiose promises ("This is sure to be a bestseller." "I know Oprah will want to feature me on her show.")

- Using cheesy graphics or tricks (printing the whole proposal on waxed paper; sending the proposal soaked in perfume; printing the proposal in different colored inks; using too many different fonts; and so on).

- Some agents and editors require a self-addressed, stamped return envelope, so include one of those (with the right amount of postage, please). If you don't, they might not even look at your proposal.

What Now?

If it is a book for the general public, send an inquiry by letter or e-mail to an agent (called a query letter). Then, if the agent likes the idea and your query letter, she will ask to see the proposal. Below is a quick tutorial about writing query letters.

THE SIX Ps TO A POWERFUL QUERY LETTER

Writing query letters is sometimes more challenging than writing your book. As in Pascal's note to a friend, "I am sorry for the length of my letter. I had not the time to write a short one." it can be difficult to boil down your 250-page book and your credentials for writing it to one page or so.

In coaching people, I have come up with a succinct formula for what should be covered in your query letter. I call it the six P method. Here are those six Ps, as succinctly as I can put them.

Purpose: Why are you contacting this particular agent or editor with this project? Did another of their authors recommend them? Have they done books that are similar to yours? Are you looking for representation on just this project or do you have more projects in mind for the future?

Position: How does this book occupy a unique position in the market (i.e., it fills an unfilled niche; its angle or slant is unique). Also, why are you the right person for the project due to your credentials and your expertise?

Population: Who, specifically, would be the likely readers of this book? It's not everybody. If the book can be more narrowly targeted to a certain definable audience, who is that (e.g., fans of John Gray; middle-age women; people on the verge of divorce)? Narrowly defining the book helps sell it and make it more marketable.

Person: Who are you? Why are you passionate about and committed to this book? How did you come to know that it should be written? Why are you the right person to write it?

Platform: This is a combination of three elements:

Portfolio: What work have you done that gives you credibility and will impress others, especially agents and editors?

Prestige: How well known are you? How motivated are your fans to buy your work? Would famous people be willing to endorse you or give you blurbs?

Promotional abilities and channels: How many people can you inform about the book in the shortest time or over time? Do you have a newsletter or an e-mail list? Do you have a radio or TV show? Do you have access to mass media on a regular basis? Are you an enthusiastic, media-savvy person who can promote your book? Do you have media training? Can you speak in sound bites? Do bookstore owners like your work based on your previous writing? Do you regularly do public speaking?

Project: What genre is this book (e.g., nonfiction self-help; chick lit; suspense; financial how-to)? What is the most succinct summary you can give of the project? This should be a summary of all the information above.

HOW DO YOU GET AN AGENT?

Another book perhaps. This one's on writing. So, enough. Stop reading. Get to work, you procrastinator. You know everything you need to know now. There's nothing stopping you. Sit down. Start writing. No excuses.

Common Writing Poisons and Their Antidotes

How to challenge unhelpful ideas or attitudes that will kill your writing dreams and ambitions.

As I have coached people on writing and publishing, I have come across the common beliefs, thoughts, and fears that have stopped people from pursuing or completing their writing. In Eastern thought this is called the "monkey mind"— always chattering but never saying anything profound or useful. I will take each poison in turn and challenge it; that is, give you an antidote. Don't feed the monkey!

Perfection

This is one that plagues many people. Either the conditions, yourself, or the writing (or all three) must be perfect before you can write or publish your work. Of course, this often stops you from even starting or at the very least makes it hard to finish. As E.B. White put it, "A writer who waits for ideal conditions under which to work will die without putting a word to paper."

To expand upon what I talked about in chapter 7, here are the variations on this poison. Take a look at them to find out if you are plagued by any of these:

- I must have a perfect setting in which to write (time, place, conditions).

- My information or knowledge must be complete and perfect.

- My writing skills must be great or perfect.

- My writing must be great or perfect—no mistakes.

- I must read another book about writing (or go to another writers' course or workshop) before I start or do a project.

- I must have the latest computer, software, or writing aid.

- Fill in your own if I haven't listed it.

I can't stress this enough. Rarely in life will the conditions, or the person, be perfect for the task. Proceed anyway. Perhaps you'll find better conditions or become a better writer along the way, but you are not likely to find those more perfect conditions unless you practice and publish.

Here are some antidotes to challenge this poison and get it out of your system or render it harmless.

ANTIDOTES

Give yourself permission to write crap or deliberately try to write badly. Many established writers don't want anyone to see their first or early drafts because they are so bad. I met songwriter and Eagles member Don Henley on a plane one time and he told me that he was asked to provide a hand-written early draft of one of his well-known songs for a book compilation and he refused because he was so embarrassed about its crappy quality.

Use a computer instead of writing freehand or on a typewriter. I honestly don't know how people finished dissertations or novels before the computer era, but obviously they somehow did. I wrote my first articles on an electric typewriter and remember with chagrin having to type the articles several times after making corrections. Boring. Frustrating. Thank the Lord for computers and word processors (I don't care if I added my small part to Bill Gates's fortune; it was well worth it). I sometimes cut out whole sections of what I have written, and I can assure myself it's okay to cut them because I will save them to a disk in case I decide I made a mistake and need that writing. It helps me take risks because it is so easy to make corrections.

I know some writers are attached to their old typewriters. But even old dogs can learn new tricks. Isaac Asimov bought some of the first word processing computers and found he could write much faster (he worked on several computers and books at once, rolling his chair between them as inspiration hit). He was fairly advanced in age when he switched to computers after writing longhand or on typewriters for many years. If he could do it, you can, too. Computers and word processing software can challenge a writer's perfectionist tendencies.

Start writing. Most good writing is rewriting anyway. Fix it in the mix, as they say in the recording business. Just get it down on paper or on the computer. Then edit and polish. It's usually much less difficult and intimidating to revise rather than stare at an empty page or blank screen.

I Don't Have Anything Original to Say

This one has never actually happened to me but I have heard it time and again from writers I have coached.

Here's the form in which this poison is usually delivered by our little monkey minds:

- It's all been said before.
- Everyone knows this already.
- I don't have anything important to say.
- Nobody will want to read it. Nobody will want to buy it.
- Who the hell am I to think I have anything to say or that I can write a book?

Trust your unique slant. Maybe what you have to say is not revolutionary or that profound, but how you say it might be. I have had people tell me after a workshop or presentation, "You know, I already knew everything you said today—but I didn't know it in this way. It finally became clear to me," or "For the first time, I think I can put this into practice." I am not insulted by this comment. I think it is usually accurate. And that may be what your writing does as well. If you can give your readers your own unique slant or take on the subject or charm them with your writing style, it won't be so crucial to be original.

Besides, it's not for you to judge. Here's what dancer/choreographer Martha Graham had to say about it and I find it inspiring and permission-giving:

> There is a vitality, a life force, an energy, a quickening that is translated through you into action—and because there is only one of you in all of time, this expression is unique. And if you block it, it will never exist through any other medium and be lost. The world will not have it. It is not your business to determine how good it is nor how it compares with other expressions. It is your business to keep it yours, clearly and directly.

I Don't Have Time to Write

Anyone who has read many books on the writing and publishing process will be familiar with the technique of writing whenever you can: early in the morning, before children or spouse awaken; during the baby's nap; on the train commuting to work; over a hasty lunch at your desk. So if you're not writing, you can't blame your kids, or your job, or lack of time.

Lack of time is one of the most common concerns or barriers I hear from would-be writers. In my writer's boot camps, I teach a process for writing in five-minute chunks. After participants learn this skill, I never hear it mentioned again. And it works—I just got an e-mail from a busy college professor who finished her book, writing in five-minute writing sessions, in less than a year.

I wrote my first ten books in ten years, with four kids at home and a full-time career (actually more than full time: I saw clients in my therapy practice about twenty hours a week, with paperwork and phone calls adding extra time to that; I did supervision with therapists in training about ten hours a week; and I traveled two or three times a month giving one- or two-day workshops). It's true that I did sleep less in those days—and I like to sleep. These days, with kids grown and gone, I sleep ten hours a night most nights. And I still get my books written and I still have a busy life.

Jodi Picoult, novelist and author of at least ten books in ten years, began writing professionally after she had her first child. In an interview with Barbara DeMarco-Barrett of the radio show *Writers on Writing*, she said, "I really learned, by the time I had three children, that I had to write in the ten minutes that they were napping or when Barney was on television or when they weren't hitting each other with a sippy cup. At any spare moment that I could, I was sitting in front of my computer and cranking something out. Now that they are more grown and I have more time, I find that discipline still serves me well."

Stephen King wrote his first novel, *Carrie*, while working full time as a schoolteacher. He had two young kids at the time. Maya Angelou tells of writing her early books with her children crawling all over her in the kitchen. There are orange juice and vomit stains on some of her early manuscripts.

I know what your mind or your fear is telling you:

- I have to make money.
- I have to raise kids.
- I have responsibilities.
- I am too tired; I am too busy.
- I will write someday when things slow down, or I go half-time, or when I'm able to slot out one day a week for my writing.

ANTIDOTE

There is only one antidote for this poison, and that is to tell yourself, as often as necessary:

Bullshit!

I trust I have convinced you that all of these reasons are just excuses or avoidance or wimpy strategies or thoughts. Don't believe them. At the end of next year, would you rather have your old thoughts and excuses or a book written?

This Will Never Get Published, So Why Bother?

Here's how the monkey mind delivers this poison:

- Lots of people have unpublished novels in their dresser drawers.

- The publishing industry is so competitive.

- I don't know anyone in publishing; I don't have an "in."

- This is a stupid dream or ambition; I'm fooling myself.

- I don't know how to get anything published.

- I was already rejected by all the publishers/agents/ magazines I tried.

- I'll fail.

The only way people ever fail totally is if they stop trying. In most areas of life, including writing and getting published, persistence pays off. Now, that doesn't mean you can just keep doing the same thing and expect it to work if it hasn't. After all, that was Albert Einstein's definition of insanity: doing the same thing over and over and expecting different results.

I used to have clients in my psychotherapy practice who had become convinced they were too boring, ugly, stupid, or unlucky to ever enter into a love relationship or marry. To cure them of this notion, I would send them to the local shopping mall. They were to observe all the couples in the mall and see how many appeared that they might be boring, ugly, stupid, or just plain weird. Invariably, there were at least a few that seemed to fit into one of those categories—yet those people somehow found someone to love or marry them. If those people could, my clients quickly realized, there was a chance for them, too. This exercise rarely failed to encourage them.

It's the same with books. Visit your local bookstore and check out some of the lame-o books that are out there. I remember reading *The Celestine Prophecy* after one of my clients urged me to read it. I thought the dialogue was wooden and the plot sucked (sorry, Mr. Redfield, but I did like your ideas if that helps at all)—but that book not only was published but became a bestseller. What a boost to my writing confidence that was! Find your own inspiration by discovering a published book that really sucks and challenge your worry or belief that you can't get published.

ANTIDOTES

Only God knows the future and what will get published. You are not God. You do the writing and put it out in the world. Let God (or fate if you don't get with the *G* word) decide what will happen. Miracles happen. Fate comes knocking at times when you don't know a way through. Like the old joke: Abe complains to God that he has been a good man all his life and has prayed to God each day for sixty years that he would win the lottery and make his miserable life a little more tolerable. In answer, he suddenly sees the heavens open and a voice booms, "Hey, Abe; help me out here—*buy a lottery ticket!*" Leave it in the hands of God or fate, but buy the lottery ticket: Write, revise, and send out your work before you decide that fate is against you.

Get some coaching or more information about how to increase the likelihood of your stuff being published. Then try again. As I mentioned above, if you are not getting published, get some help. Make your writing or your presentation better, then try again. Keep persisting and learning and honing your pitch until you sell your writing or get it published. The rewards of being published are so great that most people's doubts begin to diminish rapidly after that point. It gets even better if you begin to make money from your writing.

I have heard some novel writers say they were glad their early work was rejected, because they kept learning more by writing more and learning what editors wanted. By the time their later novels were published, they usually were doing much better work. These writers were doing two important things: They kept on learning, getting better and listening to the feedback from the world; and they persisted.

Remember, the publishing industry needs product to keep functioning. Publishers are constantly looking for publishable books and the next big thing. Somebody has to be published (there are said to be around 175,000–200,000 books published just in the United States every year). Surely there's room for your one little book in that number. They need you. If everyone gave up writing because they feared they wouldn't be published, we'd have no books.

Try writing just to write, without focusing on being published.
Madeleine L'Engle says in her book *Herself: Reflections on a Writing Life:*

> Being a writer does not necessarily mean being published. It's very nice to be published. It's what you want. When you have a vision, you want to share it. But being a writer means writing. It means building up a body of work. It means writing every day. You can hardly say that van Gogh was not a painter because he sold one painting during his lifetime, and that to his brother. But do you say that van Gogh wasn't a painter because he wasn't "published"? He was a painter because he painted, because he held true to his vision as he saw it.

One way to free yourself from this poison is to separate the writing process from being published. I've never been able to do this (I'm too product-oriented), but have heard it's a good idea, so I thought I'd throw it in. Fall in love with writing, keep writing, and you are very likely to get better as you practice it more. This in turn will make it more likely you will get published someday, but don't worry about that now. Just keep writing.

I'm Not in the Mood to Write / I'm Not Inspired

If I sit down to write when I am not inspired or visited by the Muse, the writing won't be good, so why bother, right?

Wrong! I have written a lot when I wasn't inspired. Of course, I *prefer* to be inspired; it makes everything easier. But don't wait for inspiration to strike you before you'll begin. Just get to work, and the Muse may catch up with you later.

ANTIDOTES

If you are not inspired or the writing is not coming easily, then do corrections, formatting, outlining, backups of your material or research during this noninspired time. I gather quotations, fiddle with the outline, look up key words in the dictionary, and generally do prep, editing, or correction work when I am not inspired. At least I am doing something related to my writing project and it has moved me forward.

If nothing else, make computer backups of your work during this time. I make backups on an external hard drive, to the Web, and on a little flash drive. There are never too many backups. I haven't lost a book in many years since I learned to use this noninspired time to do backups. It helps me sleep my whole ten hours very soundly, thank you.

Write anyway. The inspiration may arrive while you are writing. "Inspiration comes during work," says Madeleine L'Engle, "not before it." Back to our principle that writing begets writing: If you are writing, you will likely continue to write and eventually find the right words. Again, with computers, later you can edit or delete the words that aren't particularly inspired. For now, just get something down. Keep those fingers moving.

Write anyway. You'll exercise your writing muscle, and when the Muse deigns to visit, you'll be ready with your writing skills intact and well developed. The more you write, the better you will get. I played guitar and piano for many years at a journeyman level (not bad, but not inspired). When my skills developed to a certain level, I began to be creative, often playing things I had never played before each time I sat down to play. Well-developed writing muscles come from lots of writing. When you have a facility for writing and it comes more easily, when inspiration strikes, you will be ready to take full advantage of it.

Other People Tell Me I'm No Good

German poet Rainer Maria Rilke, in his *Letters to a Young Poet*, has a letter asking Rilke to take a look at the young poet's work and tell him whether the poems are any good and if he should go on writing them in the face of much rejection. Rilke admonishes the young man that he's asking the wrong question of the wrong person. If he has to write poetry, he should write it and critics be damned. If he can give it up, then perhaps he shouldn't be a poet. But what other people think really isn't relevant.

Nice attitude. If you can cop that one for yourself, it'll help, I think. I wrote my books because I had to. I was determined to get them published because I thought they would help others. Nothing could have stopped me, and nothing did. I just kept writing and finding ways to get my writing out to people, so I understand Rilke's advice well.

Naysayers (External and Internal)

When President John F. Kennedy announced in 1961 that the United States was committing to put a man on the moon by the end of the decade, many scientists, politicians, and citizens became excited by the prospect. They, too, committed themselves to the goal. But of course, there were naysayers. They claimed such an accomplishment was impossible (sound like some of your friends and relatives in regard to your writing dreams and goals?). But the yeasayers didn't let the naysayers stop the project. They asked a good question: What makes it impossible? Well, the naysayers replied, for one thing, there is no metal that can withstand the re-entry process without burning up. So the yeasayers got busy and found funding and researchers to solve that problem. And they solved it. Okay, the naysayers said, you solved that one; but the next one is really impossible: We don't have the computing power to make the calculations fast enough for mid-course corrections if and when the capsule goes off course. Soon the silicon chip was invented. Another problem solved. Yes, but ... said the naysayers. And so it continued until the first man walked on the moon nine years after the declaration by JFK. An old Chinese proverb advises, "The person who says it cannot be done should not interrupt the person busy doing it." Writer Jean Anouilh reminds us, "It's easy to say no. But to say yes, you have to sweat and roll up your sleeves and plunge both hands into life up to the elbows."

The point is that naysayers and skeptics and discouragers don't need to stop you. If they have worries, concerns, or barriers, let them spell them out; then you make a plan to overcome them. If they have specifics for how your writing needs to be improved or what you need to do to be successful, bring them on as helpmates. But if all they do is say it's impossible for you to write or to get published, but won't give you specifics to work with, tune them out or avoid the subject with them. Work in private until you have some published work to shut them up.

You can use the same process with the doubters and naysayers in your own head. Say, "Thank you for sharing," and go back to your writing. There's a bumper sticker I often see here in Santa Fe that reads, "Don't believe everything you think." If you have a chattering, negative monkey mind, I recommend you take this bumper sticker to heart. Vincent van Gogh, a guy who knew well troubling voices within, suggested, "If you hear a voice within you say, 'You are not a painter,' then by all means paint ... and that voice will be silenced." Crazy as he may have been, I'd say this suggestion was very sane and sensible.

Some questions to inoculate you from the unhelpful voices of discouragement:

- What do the voices (external and internal) that discourage or undermine you say about your writing and your prospects as a writer?

- What could you do to use their doubts and negativity to contribute to your writing success?

- What could you do to ignore or tune them out?

198

Key Points

- Among the poisons that can stop you or discourage you from writing or completing writing projects are: (1) need for perfection, (2) nothing to say, (3) no time, (4) never going to be published, and (5) not inspired or in the mood.

- Learn to ignore your "monkey mind" (always chattering, never helping).

- The No. 1 antidote is to *write and keep writing.*

Bonus: How Not to Get Yourself to Write a Book

- Don't write. Do anything and everything but write. Go to writers conferences. Read writing books. Think about writing. Think that you can't write.

- Don't write. Wait until you are inspired or in the mood to write.

- Don't listen to anyone. Don't get edited. Never show anyone your writing. If you do, don't take any advice. Don't listen to anyone's suggestions about how to improve your writing or your book.

- Listen to everyone. Take to heart everyone's opinion about your writing or whether you can write a book. Believe everything you think, especially the discouraging thoughts or beliefs that stop you from writing or putting your work out into the world.

- Keep it to yourself. Don't send your work out to be published.

- Don't write. (Is this sounding familiar?) Give up writing or trying to get published.

Index

visibility of author.
See platform
Vonnegut, Kurt, 43

W

TheWashingtonienne
(Cutler), 78
Watson, Thomas, Jr., 127
Web sites of authors, 144–145
Weiner-Davis, Michele, 170
What About Bob? (movie), 74
White, E. B., 185
Winspear, Jacqueline, 67
WordPress, 79
workshops, 15, 35–36,
62–63, 67
writer's block, 45–47, 84, 134
Writer's Digest (magazine), 7
Writers on Writing (radio
show), 189
writing patterns
body position and move-
ment, 60
discovering, 54–56

duration of sessions, 57–58
experimenting with, 61–64
mode of writing, 60
overview, 52–54
people and, 58–59
points of entry, 60–61
setting, 56–57
sharing your work, 59
timing, 57
tools (telephones, e-mail,
etc.), 58
viewing and doing, 61
writing to write, 36, 80, 194

Y

YouTube.com, 145

Z

Zen and the Art of Writing
(Bradbury), 11
Zen of Writing principle,
36, 80, 194
Zinsser, William, 156

Worksheet Index

WORKSHEETS FOUND IN THIS BOOK AND ON THE DVD

DVD Exclusive Handouts

HANDOUTS FROM BILL'S WORKSHOPS

- Handout 1: The 10 Ps to Getting Your Book Written & Published
- Handout 2: How to Research the Market & the Competition
- Handout 3: Crafting an Origin Story
- Handout 4: Four Essential Nonfiction Book Proposal Elements
- Handout 5: How to Get an Agent
- Handout 6: The Money & Legal Stuff About Trade Books

About the DVD

Because Bill's forte is public speaking, we have included a DVD that allows you to experience one of his writing and publishing boot camps.

We also have included the worksheets in this book on the DVD (in PDF form), as well as some audio programs from Bill's podcast. We are trying to get to you in as many modalities as possible (reading, listening, watching) to ensure your writing success. It will work in any DVD player or computer with a DVD player.

The minimum Windows system requirements for playing enhanced DVD discs include:

- Windows 98SE, ME, 2000, XP
- Internet Explorer 5.0
- DirectX 7.0
- Intel Celeron/Pentium or AMD Duron/Athlon processor, 400MHz
- 64 MB of RAM (2000 and XP: 128 MB of RAM)
- 4 MB graphics card, 800 x 600 resolution, 16-bit color
- Direct Sound compatible sound card
- 4X DVD-ROM drive (UDMA enabled)
- Direct Show compliant DVD decoder software
- Adobe Reader (version 7.0)

The minimum Macintosh system requirements for playing enhanced DVD discs include:

- Mac OS X 10.3 (Panther)
- Safari 1.1 or later, or Internet Explorer for Mac OS X 5.2 or later
- Power Mac G3, G4, or G5, iMac, eMac, PowerBook G3 or G4, or iBook (with 128 MB or RAM)
- Built-in Firewire
- Internal DVD-ROM drive (external DVD-ROM drives are not supported)
- DVD playback capability with the Apple DVD Player
- Adobe Preview (version 3.0.1)

Note: The original PowerBook G3 and processor upgrade cards are not supported.

This DVD may not be compatible with all Mac or PC computer DVD drives. Check system requirements. DVD should be compatible for all consumer DVD players.

WRITE IS A VERB